D0616850

DOROTHY DAY

DOROTHY DAY

IN MY OWN WORDS

Edited and Compiled
by Phyllis Zagano

Liguori
LIGUORI, MISSOURI

Imprimi Potest:
Richard Thibodeau, C.Ss.R.
Provincial, Denver Province
The Redemptorists

Published by Liguori Publications
Liguori, Missouri
www.liguori.org
www.catholicbooksonline.com

Compilation and Introduction copyright 2003
by Phyllis Zagano

Library of Congress Cataloging-in-Publication Data

Day, Dorothy, 1987–1980.
 Dorothy Day : in my own words / compiled by Phyllis Zagano.—1st ed.
  p. cm.
 Includes bibliographical references.
 ISBN 0-7648-0926-1
 1. Catholic Church—Charities. 2. Church and social problems—Catholic Church. 3. Catholic Worker Movement. I. Zagano, Phyllis. II. Title.

BX2182.3 .D39 2003
267'.182—dc21   2002031275

Interior photographs on pages 1, 35, 69, and 87: Marquette University Archives; page 101: Bill Barrett. Used with permission.

Printed in the United States of America
07 06 05 04 03   5 4 3 2 1
First edition

For Paul L. Zagano

CONTENTS

PREFACE ix

INTRODUCTION xi

Part One
   The Thirties: Founding the
   Movement 1

Part Two
   The Forties: The War Years 35

Part Three
   The Fifties: Pacifism and the Atomic
   Bomb 69

Part Four
   The Sixties: Civil Rights and Civil
   Disobedience 87

Part Five
   The Seventies: The
   Pilgrimage Continued 101

BIBLIOGRAPHY 117

$\mathcal{P}$REFACE

Books don't just happen. This book is the result of an invitation by Judy Bauer and Bob Byrns of Liguori Publications to read the works of Dorothy Day for short bits of her wisdom to pass along. Much of that reading was done in the library at Marymount College, Tarrytown. It is to the Marymount librarians, especially Sister Saint Edward McLaughlin, R.S.H.M., Sister Mary Elizabeth Rathgeb, R.S.H.M., and JoEllen Morrison, as well as to former library director David Oettinger, that I owe the greatest debt for both research assistance and good cheer as I continued the endeavor. Ann Louise Williams kept my typing and my editing on the straight and narrow.

This new century has new challenges to new servants of the Body of Christ. The new-old ulcers of war and poverty cry out for healing of the sort Dorothy Day managed to both recommend and give. May this book somehow help restart the healing, and help those who are able continue the salving of wounds too personal and too deep for any but their owners to understand. May it, through the words of Dorothy Day, help stop for one minute, or one hour, or even forever, the sort of evils that she saw so clearly and so well.

I have dedicated this book to my father, whose life overlapped much of Dorothy Day's and whose memories of Brooklyn during the Depression and of World War II colored in for me her black-and-white renditions of the times.

$\mathcal{I}$ NTRODUCTION

The Lower East Side that Dorothy Day served does not seem that different now from the way she described it fifty or sixty years ago.

On a hot August afternoon, the patchwork quilt of faces passing by—every shade of brown and red and yellow and tan—is a striking reminder of the human tide of suffering she met there every day. Each language of the globe echoes on Third Street, where Maryhouse still sits proudly in the late day sun. Farther downtown, boys in swim trunks try to beat the line by climbing the fence to the public pool; their older sisters roll their eyes in embarrassment. Mothers drag small ones to the market for the day's meal with the day's wage. Fathers in construction pound at pavement, glad of a good job and hopeful of some coolness in the evening. The tiredness in every eye is not from heat and not from work, but from the daily and relentless grind of poverty in a section of New York surrounded by unimaginable wealth.

It is hard to walk those streets and do nothing. But the heat and the other duties of the day press in until those sad eyes are forgotten, unless someone else reminds us.

Dorothy Day reminds us. Dorothy Day will not let anyone forget. She railed against it all when she was alive, and her words continue to remind us now. She railed against it all, but mostly she railed against the rich who ignored the poor. All kinds of rich people. All kinds of poor people. She especially chided those who could not apply, who could not live, the works of mercy every single day.

We might like to turn away from what she says. We might like to complain that all this talk about the poor gets repetitive, tiresome. Perhaps that is the point. There is nothing so repetitive, nothing so tiresome, as poverty. But the poor cannot simply turn the page on it.

Dorothy Day was born in Brooklyn, New York, in 1897. She was the third of five children of parents whose marriage symbolically reunited the fractured continent, split as it had been by the Civil War between the Confederacy and the Union. Her father was a sportswriter from the South whose own father was a Confederate Army surgeon. Her mother was a Northerner, from the Upper Hudson Valley and Massachusetts. The family traveled with her journalist father; Dorothy remembered the 1906 San Francisco earthquake, and her mother helping its victims. Dorothy lived for a time in Brooklyn, and in New York State along the Hudson; one of her earliest memories include walking across the frozen river. She finished high school in Chicago at sixteen and then attended the University of Illinois at Urbana, where she joined the Socialist Party in 1914. By 1916, she arrived in New York to begin her career as a writer, starting at the Socialist daily newspaper, *The Call*, while carrying the union card of the Industrial Workers of the World. Soon she was working at *The Masses* with John Reed and Max Eastman, but the government suppressed the publication for sedition. As World War I continued, she went to Washington, D.C., to march with suffragists in 1917, and ended up in jail. Back in New York's Greenwich Village, she became an inseparable companion of playwright Eugene O'Neill, but broke from his circle of friends when one of their number committed suicide. All the while, however, she maintained a bohemian life—distrustful of structure and religion. At twenty-two, following a failed relationship with a much older man while working as a nurse at Kings County Hospital, Brooklyn, she had an abortion.

She traveled from job to job, writing for *The Liberator* (the successor to *The Masses*). The novel she was always writing turned into an autobiographical novel, *The Eleventh Virgin*. When she sold the movie rights for $5,000 she was able to buy a small bungalow facing the water in then-rural Staten Island, just a ferry ride away from Manhattan. There she lived her brief common-law marriage to biologist Forster Batterham and remained in that small house, with their child Tamar Teresa, after he left her.

Catholicism was one reason for the split; Dorothy had met a Sister Aloysius on the beach, whose tutoring brought Dorothy from Anglicanism into the Roman Catholic Church. Her conversion was powerful, but not peaceful. Dorothy anguished over leaving her identity with the poor to join the Church of power, wealth, and privilege.

She also had to earn a living. For a while she read novels for the film company Metro-Goldwyn-Mayer, earning six dollars for every summary she turned in. As the twenties roared on, she found herself invited to the privileged life of a Hollywood writer. With Tamar, she took a train to Los Angeles and a $125 per week job writing film scripts for the Pathé studio. The job lasted three months. She and Tamar went to Mexico, from

which Dorothy filed stories for the lay Catholic magazine *Commonweal*. Their quick return was precipitated by Tamar's bout with malaria.

The New York they had left was blighted by the Great Depression when they returned in 1930, and Dorothy's faith and devotion deepened with every passing day. Around this time she began to attend daily Mass. Day by difficult day, her radicalism became a radical Christianity, and her life turned into total self-donation to the poor. Her writing career began to become her vocation as a writer. In 1932, she met Peter Maurin, an itinerant philosopher whose theories of personalism she put into action. Good was to be done not by large institutions for the masses, but singly and individually, for real people, one by simple one. With Maurin she founded the Catholic Worker Movement, and soon after its newspaper, *The Catholic Worker*. The first issue proclaimed why:

To Our Readers

For those who are sitting on park benches in the warm spring sunlight.

For those who are huddling in shelters trying to escape the rain.

For those who are walking the streets in the all but futile search for work.

For those who think that there is no hope for

the future, no recognition of their plight—this little paper is addressed.

It is printed to call their attention to the fact that the Catholic Church has a social program— to let them know that there are men of God who are working not only for their spiritual but also their material welfare.

Filling a Need

It's time there was a Catholic paper printed for the unemployed.

The fundamental aim of most radical sheets is the conversion of its readers to radicalism and atheism.

Is it not possible to be radical and not atheist?

Is it not possible to protest, to expose, to complain, to point out abuses and demand reforms without desiring the overthrow of religion?

In an attempt to popularize and make known the encyclicals of the Popes in regard to social justice and the program put forth by the Church for the "reconstruction of the social order," this news sheet, The Catholic Worker, is started.

THE CATHOLIC WORKER, MAY 1, 1933.

That May Day, 1933, twenty-five hundred copies of *The Catholic Worker* appeared, distributed one by one by hand. Landing squarely in the midst of the Great Depression, the paper proclaimed not so much the rights of workers but their right to dignity. It also argued from the start for the unique majesty of every single human person, each worker, wife, and child, and for their right to fairness, justice, and honest treatment by industry and government, landlords, and neighbors. It argued, with prescient clarity, that we are all in this together.

The first House of Hospitality opened its arms to people in need in 1933. Dorothy's daughter, Tamar, was seven and lived there with her mother. By now, Dorothy was wholly involved in the movement to expand the works of mercy to become an everyday way of being. In 1935, the concept of communal sharing of life and time with the poor grew to include a twelve-room house with a garden on Staten Island, not far from Dorothy's little beach bungalow. That project was replaced by "Maryfarm" in Easton, Pennsylvania, where Peter Maurin repaired to argue philosophy with its residents and where Dorothy often visited. The first farm was soon mirrored by a second down the road.

As the works of mercy continued, Dorothy's writing maintained its radical tone. She objected, and objected strongly, to the way Spanish Catholics justified the Spanish Civil War. She was more concerned about the plight of the workers in the face of Franco's anti-Communism. While *The Catholic Worker* maintained its pacifist stance throughout this war and the Second World War that ensued, *The Catholic Worker* circulation fell from 190,000 in 1938 to 50,000 by the war's end.

The economic stances of *The Catholic Worker* in the 1930s, however, obscured for most its religious roots. Catholic Worker socialism—really an economic voluntarism—was truly the "Christian communism," as Peter Maurin called it. The argument was for "worker ownership of the means of production and distribution as distinguished from nationalization," as Dorothy explained. The distinct understanding of personalism espoused by the movement was often overtaken by the fact that its stance was indistinguishable from anarchism. Even so, the Catholic Worker Movement could not be said to oppose all organization, only the organization of whatever sort that depersonalized the individual. It was during this first decade of the Catholic Worker that the group opened various residences and successful houses of hospitality in lower Manhattan, and at least one failed house in Harlem. Throughout the decade, Dorothy relentlessly reminded readers of the class distinctions so readily apparent between those who controlled production and distribution and those who produced and distributed, even suggesting that the growing prospect of war was one more economic opportunity for the rich.

Dorothy Day and Peter Maurin separately traveled around the country during the Depression giving talks—in Washington, in Los Angeles, in Cleveland—after which a house of hospitality might spring up, inspired by the cause. The very real and pressing project, whether in Milwaukee or Boston or Portland, was to feed and house the workers who, for a time at least, had nowhere else to go.

Dorothy wrote about her life again in 1942 in her book *From Union Square to Rome*, which traced both passageways and connections between her economic and religious beliefs. It was at the end, however, all about love. She wrote:

> But it is hard to understand the love of God for us. We pray daily to increase in the love of God because we know that if we love a person very much, all things become easy to us and delightful. We want, rather unreasonably, sensible feelings of love. Saint Teresa says that the only way we can measure the love we have for God is the love we have for our fellows. So by working for our fellows we come to love them. That

you understand, for you believe that you are
working for them when you give hours
every morning to the distribution of
literature, climbing tenement-house stairs,
knocking at doors, suffering rebuffs, enduring heat and cold, weariness and hardship,
to bring to them what you consider a gospel
which will set them free.

And if you and I love our faulty fellow
human beings, how much more must God
love us all? If we as human parents can
forgive our children any neglect, any crime,
and work and pray patiently to make them
better, how much more does God love us?

FROM UNION SQUARE TO ROME

As the 1930s turned into the 1940s, and the
prospect of war became a reality, Dorothy wrote
somewhat ambivalently about Americans who
joined the war effort, and then looked kindly on
those who returned, looking, searching, always
hoping, for work. No matter to her pacifist stance,
they had lain down their lives for others. The new
economic struggles of the post-war years brought
the old problems back to Lower Manhattan. *The
Catholic Worker*'s pacifist stance had decimated
the paper's circulation; bulk subscriptions to
parishes and institutions fell drastically, although

individual subscriptions remained relatively stable. During the war, many Catholic Worker Houses of Hospitality had to close, due to lack of personnel, and the upper and lower farms in Pennsylvania fell on hard times as well. The lower farm lasted until 1946, the upper until 1949.

Waves of anti-communism crashed over *The Catholic Worker* during the "Red scare" years of the 1950s. The newspaper took up the cause of spies Julius and Ethel Rosenberg, and Dorothy wrote about their execution just a few miles down the Hudson River from where she was at the replacement Maryfarm on a warm June evening. "Let us have no part of the vindictive State," she wrote against the tide, sympathetic not so much to their cause but to the fact that they believed so deeply in it. Her combined pro-labor and anti-war stance caused her to be labeled a Communist by many, but she never pulled up her radical roots in Christianity. If anything, as years turned into decades, those roots grew deeper and her faith flourished even more. She was more than willing to stand up against "the establishment"—in fact, against any establishment, secular or religious, that wavered from her understanding of the gospel, and that did not appear at least to take the works of mercy as seriously as she did.

Through the 1950s, when the United States

became involved in the Korean War, to the 1960s when Vietnam loomed ahead, and into the 1970s, Dorothy Day retained her pacifist stance and continued her travels and her writings. With a group of other women, she fasted for ten days at the Second Vatican Council in Rome, in an effort to get the Council to condemn all war. It did condemn nuclear war. She was instrumental in the founding of Pax Christi, USA, and *The Catholic Worker* was the first Catholic publication to advocate civil disobedience in opposition to the Vietnam Conflict. In 1965, draft-card burning became a crime punishable by up to five years in jail. Catholic Worker activists organized public burnings, and went to jail. When a Catholic Worker named Roger LaPorte committed suicide by lighting gasoline he had poured over himself while sitting cross-legged in front of the United Nations buildings in Manhattan, the Catholic Worker Movement, newspaper, and very concept became the target of very real religious and secular criticism. Some even blamed Dorothy Day directly for the violence done in the name of pacifism, but she denied the link. She also denied the violent actions of Jesuit anti-war activist Daniel Berrigan and the Catonsville Nine, who raided and damaged draft-board offices in Catonsville, Maryland, explaining later that violence done now to objects would lead inevitably to violence to persons. Even so, when one day in 1968 Berrigan celebrated Mass at Saint Joseph's House of Hospitality, Dorothy declared that the way to end "this insane war" was to "pack the jails with our men."

Dorothy Day's work and her life cannot be characterized, because they comprised so much of the unpredictable predictability of the gospel. She was a mother, and a grandmother nine times over. She received visitors and corresponded often beyond the limits of her strength. Her determinations and decisions were rooted in her deep religious sensibilities. She did not disrespect organized religion, but neither would she bend when she saw its excesses. During a public television interview late in life, she decried the riches of religious orders, whose seminaries and novitiates along the Hudson River marked a wealth she could not square with gospel teachings. Her criticism was deemed caustic by some, but her aim never wavered. Her determined voluntary poverty continued to grow, and included the Catholic Worker Movement itself: she steadfastly refused to register it as a non-profit agency, eschewing both status and tax advantage.

Throughout, Dorothy retained and strengthened her vocation as a writer. She wrote over

1,000 articles for *The Catholic Worker*, and 350 more for other publications. Seven books tumbled out of her typewriter after her first, the autobiographical novel *The Eleventh Virgin* (1924). Most were about her work. *House of Hospitality* (1939), *From Union Square to Rome* (1942), *On Pilgrimage* (1948), *The Long Loneliness* (1952), *Thérèse* (1960), her biography of Saint Thérèse of Lisieux, and *Loaves and Fishes* (1963) were joined late in her life by an anthology of her *Catholic Worker* columns, *On Pilgrimage: The Sixties* (1972). Manuscripts of three additional books, "The Dispossessed" (1932, 1946), "Peter Maurin" (1948), and "All Is Grace" (1959–1975) are held at the Marquette University Archives.

When the century and Dorothy were both in their seventies, she picketed with United Farm Worker activist Cesar Chavez, fought with the Internal Revenue Service over status of *The Catholic Worker*, and received the Laetare Medal from the University of Notre Dame. On August 6, 1976, the thirty-first anniversary of Hiroshima, Dorothy Day made her last public speech at the forty-first International Eucharistic Congress in Philadelphia. It was an event that brought together Mother Teresa, Cardinal Karol Wojtyla (Pope John Paul II), and U.S. President Gerald Ford, among others. She had a heart attack that evening and never regained her strength. She died on November 29, 1980, at Maryhouse on the Lower East Side of Manhattan. Her daughter, Tamar, was with her.

Dorothy Day had spent her life serving God's people, and now she was with God. At the Catholic Worker farm in Tivoli, it is said she was always in one of two places: the chapel or with visitors. In chapel, she had long lists of people she was praying for. Outside chapel, she was sharing coffee, conversation, and the very fabric of her life. And people no doubt prayed for her. Now people pray to her, and she is on her way to formal declaration as a saint. Dorothy Day did not like being called a saint. She said she did not wish to be dismissed so easily. Nevertheless, John Cardinal O'Connor, Archbishop of New York, introduced the cause for her canonization in 2000, calling her "a modern day devoted daughter of the Church" and a "model for all in the third millennium."

Her gravestone has on it some loaves and fishes and the words "*Deo Gratias*."

* * *

What follows is a collection of writings of Dorothy Day, the twentieth-century Catholic activist (and, I would say, apostle), who founded The Catholic

Worker. *The Church now calls her "Servant of God"; in her time, she was the conscience of her city.*

Long and short selections from her writings follow, in the chronological order of their creation, selected with an eye toward her delineation of the corporal and spiritual works of mercy.

This text is reprinted from "Dorothy Day Library on the Web" at URL: http://www.catholicworker.org/dorothyday/ and is not copyrighted. However, if you use or cite this text please indicate the original publication source and this website. Thank you.

Part One

THE THIRTIES: FOUNDING THE MOVEMENT

The Works of Mercy

The early Christians started with the works of mercy and it was this technique which converted the world. They run in this wise: The corporal works—to feed the hungry; to give drink to the thirsty; to clothe the naked; to harbor the harborless; to ransom the captive; to visit the sick; to bury the dead.

The spiritual works are—to instruct the ignorant; to counsel the doubtful; to admonish sinners; to bear wrongs patiently; to forgive offense willingly; to comfort the afflicted; to pray for the living and the dead.

Not all of these works are within the reach of all—that is understood. But that we should take part in some of them is a matter of obligation, a "strict precept imposed both by the natural and Divine law."

THE CATHOLIC WORKER, FEBRUARY 1935

Shoestring Start-Up

*I*n an attempt to popularize and make known the encyclicals of the Popes, in regard to social justice and the program put forth by the Church for the "reconstruction of the social order," this news sheet, *The Catholic Worker*, is started....

This first number of *The Catholic Worker* was planned, written and edited in the kitchen of a tenement on Fifteenth Street, on subway platforms, on the "L," the ferry. There is no editorial office, no overhead in the way of telephone or electricity, no salaries paid.

The money for the printing of the first issue was raised by begging small contributions from friends. A colored priest in Newark sent us ten dollars and the prayers of his congregation. A colored sister in New Jersey, garbed also in holy poverty, sent us a dollar. Another kindly and generous friend sent twenty-five. The rest of it the editors squeezed out of their own earnings, and at that they were using money necessary to pay milk bills, gas bills, electric light bills.

THE CATHOLIC WORKER, MAY 1933

No Place to Lay His Head

*I*t is cheering to remember that Jesus Christ wandered this earth with no place to lay his head. The foxes have holes and the birds of the air their nests, but the Son of Man has no place to lay his head. And when we consider our fly-by-night existence, our uncertainty, we remember (with pride at sharing the honor) that the disciples supped by the seashore and wandered through cornfields picking the ears from the stalks wherewith to make their frugal meals.

THE CATHOLIC WORKER, MAY 1933

Minus a Meal?

"*G*ermans to pare one meal a month to feed jobless" is another headline. Yesterday, while I wandered around town to view the parade, I was disheartened at the sight of so many women in the tea shops and luncheon places, spending so much money on so little, and eating so many unnecessary things when so many are going hungry. It wouldn't hurt any of them to practice *agere contra* when they are tempted to indulge in an orgy of sweets. The Germans are going to pare one meal a month off their diet. Why can't we go them one better, or four better, and pare off one meal a week and give that money to charity? Or not even one meal, but one afternoon tea, which usually comes to fifty or sixty cents.

THE CATHOLIC WORKER, OCTOBER 1933

Families Fare Worse Than Pigs

A deer gets trapped on a hillside and every effort is brought to bear to rescue him from his predicament. The newspapers carry daily features. Three little pigs are crowded into a too-small cage, the case is brought into court, the judge's findings in the case being that pigs should not be crowded the way subway riders are. And a family of eight children, mother, and father are crowded in three rooms and the consensus of opinion is that they're lucky to have that and why don't they practice birth control anyway.

THE CATHOLIC WORKER, NOVEMBER 1933

Neat But Still Needy

A few weeks ago I went over to Saint Zita's to see a sister there and the woman who answered the door took it for granted that I came to beg for shelter. The same morning I dropped into the armory on Fourteenth Street, where lunches are being served to unemployed women, and there they again motioned me into the waiting room, thinking that I had come for food. These incidents are significant. After all my heels are not run down—my clothes were neat—I am [like the] girls, and women, who to the average eye, look as though they came from comfortable surroundings are really homeless and destitute.

You see them in the waiting rooms of all the department stores. To all appearances they are waiting to meet their friends, to go on a shopping tour—to a matinee, or to a nicely served lunch in the store restaurant. But in reality they are looking for work (you can see the worn newspapers they leave behind with the help-wanted page well thumbed), and they have no place to go, no place to rest but in these public places—and no good hot lunch to look forward to. The stores are thronged with women buying dainty underwear which they could easily do without—compacts for a dollar, when the cosmetics in the five-and-ten are just as good—and mingling with these protected women and often indistinguishable from them are these sad ones, these desolate ones, with no homes, no jobs, and never enough food in their stomachs.

THE CATHOLIC WORKER, JUNE 1934

Saint Teresa of Ávila's Struggle With Sin

Saint Teresa [of Ávila] struggled for twenty years, she said, to avoid the occasions of sin. To know what she was talking about, what she meant by sin, it is necessary to understand the situation she was in.

She had entered the convent at the age of eighteen. The Carmelite convent was a large one, containing so many nuns that it was difficult to feed them all. It was the custom of the day to send unmarried daughters, widows, ladies who wished to retire from the world, to the convent and yet they did not retire from the world. There were a great many visitors. Saint Teresa herself said that one of the reasons so many visitors came was to bring food to the nuns, and they received their callers because there was so little food in the convent that they needed to eke out their re-sources in that way. Later when Saint Teresa was making her foundations of the reformed Carmelites, she saw to it that her nuns had enough to eat.

Saint Teresa knew that she was far from leading the life she wished to lead when she entered the convent. She wished to give herself up wholly to God. She wished everything she did, every word she said, to tend to that end. But she was a gay creature. The story is that she went to be received in the convent in a bright red dress. She was full of vitality, life. She wished to live abundantly. The very qualities in her which urged her to give herself to God drew her to her fellows. She had an abundant love for them, an interest in them, and there was much time spent in conver-sations.

The more her life was involved with her fellows, the more she was drawn to them, the more she felt she was drawing away from God....

But Saint Teresa had so great a desire for perfection that any time engaged in idle talk (the most innocent idle talk) seemed to her to be deliberately stolen from God. She knew what she wanted, she knew that there was a better life for her, but she had a struggle to attain it.

She tells...how she was kept from prayer. "The

sadness I felt on entering the oratory was so great that it required all the courage I had to force myself in. They say of me that my courage is not slight, and it is known that God has given me a courage beyond that of a woman; but I have made a bad use of it."

She told, too, of watching the hour glass, of how she was filled with distractions, of what a constant hard struggle it was to force herself to prayer and spiritual reading. And these struggles went on for twenty years!

"I wished to live," she wrote, "but I saw clearly that I was not living, but rather wrestling with the shadow of death; there was no one to give me life, and I was not able to take it."

The shadow of death she was talking of was the life she was leading, purposeless, disordered, a constant succumbing to second-best, to the less-than-perfect which she desired. But human nature will try to persuade us that the life of prayer is death, is a turning away from life.

AMERICA MAGAZINE, AUGUST 4, 1934

Letter to an Agnostic

As a convert I can say these things, knowing how many times I turned away, almost in disgust, from the idea of God and giving myself up to him.

I know the feeling of uneasiness, of weariness, the feeling of strain put upon the soul from driving it, instead of abandoning it to God. And how anyone can persist in the search for God without the assistance of the Church and the advice of her confessors, with the experience of generations behind them, I do not know.

The thing you do not understand is the elemental fact that our beginning and our last end is God. Once that fact is accepted, half the struggle is won. If we wish to go on struggling, not to be content with the minimum of virtue, of duty done, of "just getting by," then we should account it a great honor that God has given us these desires, to serve him and to use ourselves completely in his service.

You do not see this, you do not believe it. Every now and then, when you think of religion in your busy life, you end by turning from it with aversion.

You are very young, scarcely twenty-one, and you have not yet really felt the need, the yearning toward God.

You have not been in such agony and misery that you turned to One whom you knew not and said: "God help me!" Or if you did, you were ashamed of doing it afterward, feeling it to be cowardice to turn in misery to a God in whom you did not believe.

I felt this despair when I lay in jail for fifteen days (after demonstrating for the rights of political prisoners), contemplating the fundamental misery of human existence, a misery which would remain even if social justice were achieved and a state of Utopia prevailed. For you cannot pace the floor of a barred cell, or lie on your back on a hard cot watching a gleam of sunlight travel slowly, oh, so slowly, across the room, without coming to the realization that until the heart and soul of man is changed, there is no hope of happiness for him....

You do not know how long I struggled. How I turned to God, and turned from him, again and again; I, too, felt that distaste, I, too, felt that religion had a morbid quality.

It is the struggle of the flesh against the spirit. It is the struggle of the natural man against that in him that is Divine.

AMERICA MAGAZINE, AUGUST 4, 1934

Wise Counsels

We have "a rule of life" which is easy to follow, provided we listen to the wise counsels of such people as Saint Teresa, Saint Francis de Sales, de Caussade, Father Considine. I mention these names because they are the first ones that come to mind who have been of help this past year.

Saint Teresa understood that weariness of the soul; Saint Francis tells us to be gentle with ourselves; de Caussade tells us to abandon ourselves to Divine Providence, and Father Considine tells us to have more faith in God as a kind Father who is so far above our earthly fathers that he will forgive us all our sins, even the greatest, who will not give us a stone when we ask for bread.

We are taught that our souls need exercise just as our body does, otherwise it will never be healthy and well, and if it is not a healthy state, of course we will feel morbid. And prayer is that exercise for the soul, just as bending and stretching is the exercise of the body. It is intellectual pride, the arrogance of youth which makes the physical act of prayer difficult.

AMERICA MAGAZINE, AUGUST 4, 1934

Sacramental Cannibalism

*Y*ou say you object to religion because it has a cannibalistic aspect which revolts you. A twelve-year-old girl who was brought up with no knowledge of the Christian religion said almost the same thing to me last winter.

"Catholics believe that they eat the Body and Blood of Christ, don't they?" she said, with a look of distaste. She, too, did not mean to blaspheme. She was honest. And I'm going to send this letter to her, too, when I have finished it.

I suppose I never felt this objection, this repulsion, because long before I became a radical I had felt deeply the Mysteries of faith, not the Faith, but faith nevertheless. I read the Bible when I was twelve, and Wesley's sermons, picked up in a secondhand store, uplifted my soul to God and I knew what my conscience was and what was good and evil. I had once accepted the doctrine of the Holy Eucharist. So when I came back to God there was not that difficulty to overcome.

THE CATHOLIC WORKER, SEPTEMBER 1934

A Simple Mystery

*T*his teaching, that Christ would be their daily bread, was so simple, so elemental a thing, in spite of its mystery that children and the simplest and least of people in the world could understand and accept it.

Saint Teresa says that Christ is disguised as bread so that we will not fear to approach Him— so that we can go to him in confidence, daily, needing him daily as we need our physical bread.

We are not, most of us, capable of exalted emotion, save rarely. We are not capable of feelings of love, awe, gratitude, and repentance. So Christ has taken the form of bread that we may more readily approach Him, and feeding daily, assimilating Christ so that it is not we but Christ working in us, we become more capable of understanding and realizing and loving Him.

Yes, in bread, Christ has become so simple— has condescended so far that a child, a savage, can understand and eat the sacred food with love and gratitude…. And even the nearest and dearest of his friends were dispersed and fled, not understanding or realizing the mystery of the Redemption, how Christ was laying down his life for all men.

When he prayed in agony in the garden—

when all the weight of sins descended upon him, all the sins that had been and that would be committed throughout the world forever after; when he suffered all the temptations, all the horror, all the remorse for the rest of the world— his disciples did not understand that either. He watched and suffered in his agony and prayed. He had told them that the next day he was to die. And in spite of his miracles they paid so little attention to his words that they slept, as the friend they loved most in the world struggled against the thought of his death. They left him alone, they slept, and the next day they all fled so little did they understand his teachings, though they had been with him for three years and listened to his talk.

They did not understand even after they had eaten with him at the Last Supper. They did not understand until the Holy Spirit descended upon them and it was given to them to understand.

So how can I understand or try to tell you about it? If they who lived with him, who could see him as man, eat with him, sleep with him, and wander with him through the countryside, if they were "offended" and dispersed, how can I try to tell you what is in my heart? I do not ask myself, "How can I try to overcome your objection?" Only God can do that. I am not trying to convert you, but just trying not to let go unchallenged your objections, for fear that my not answering would seem to you a kind of denial of him whom I love.

There is the question, why did Christ institute this Sacrament of his Body and Blood? And the answer is very simple. It was because he loved us and wished to be with us. "My delights are to be with the children of men." He made us and he loved us. His presence in the Blessed Sacrament is the great proof of that love.

THE CATHOLIC WORKER, SEPTEMBER 1934

The Humanity of Jesus Christ

Saint Teresa of Ávila said that we should meditate more on the love of God for us, rather than our love for him. And she emphasizes his sacred humanity and says that by never losing sight of that it is easier for us to realize that love. She is always talking about the Man Jesus.

But it is hard to understand the love of God for us. We pray daily to increase in the love of God, because we know that if we love a person very much, all things become easy to us and delightful. We want, rather unreasonably, sensible feelings of love. Saint Teresa says that the only way we can measure the love we have for God is the love we have for our fellows. So by working for our fellows we come to love them. That you understand, for you believe that you are working for them when you give hours every morning to the distribution of literature, climbing tenement-house stairs, knocking at doors, suffering rebuffs, enduring heat and cold, weariness and hardship, to bring to them what you consider a gospel which will set them free.

And if you and I love our faulty fellow-human beings, how much more must God love us all? If we as human parents can forgive our children any neglect, any crime, and work and pray patiently to make them better, how much more does God love us?

You may say perhaps: "How do we know he does, if there is a he!" And I can only answer that we know it because he is here present with us today in the Blessed Sacrament on the altar, that he never has left us, that by daily going to him for the gift of himself as daily bread, I am convinced of that love. I have the faith that feeding at that table has nourished my soul so that there is life in it, and a lively realization that there is such a thing as the love of Christ for us.

It took me a long time as a convert to realize the presence of Christ as Man in the Sacrament. He is the same Jesus who walked on earth, who slept in the boat as the tempest arose, who hungered in the desert, who prayed in the garden, who conversed with the woman by the well, who rested at the house of Martha and Mary, who wandered through the cornfields, picking the ears of corn to eat.

Jesus is there as Man. He is there, flesh and blood, soul and Divinity. He is our leader who is always with us. Do you wonder that Catholics are exultant in this knowledge, that their leader is with them? "I shall be with you always, even to the end of the world."

Christ is bread on our altars because bread is the staple of the world, the simplest thing in the world, something of which we eat and never get tired. We will always have bread whether it is corn, wheat, or rye, or whatever it is made from. We will always find wherever we go some staple which is called bread.

We eat to sustain life; it is the most elemental thing we do. For the life of the body we need food. For the life of the soul we need food. So the simplest, most loving, most thorough, thing Christ could do before he died was to institute the Blessed Sacrament and hold up bread and say, "This is my body," and wine and say, "This my blood; take and eat. Do this in commemoration of me." If you sat and thought forever and ever, you

could not think of any way for Christ to remain
with us, which would bring us closer to him.

THE CATHOLIC WORKER, SEPTEMBER 1934

Revolution

We have all probably noted those sudden
moments of quiet—those strange and almost
miraculous moments in the life of a big city when
there is a cessation of traffic noises—just an
instant when there is only the sound of footsteps
which serves to emphasize a sudden peace. During
those seconds it is possible to notice the sunlight,
to notice our fellow humans, to take breath.

After hours of excitement and action and
many human contacts, when even in one's sleep
and at moments of waking there is a sense of the
imminence of things to be done and of conflict
ahead, it is good to seek those moments of perfect
stillness and refreshment during early Mass.

Then indeed it seems that God touches the
heart and the mind. There are moments of
recollection, of realization when the path seems
straighter, the course to be followed perfectly
plain, though not easy. It is as though the great
Physician to whom we go for healing had put
straight that which was dislocated, and prescribed

a course of action so definite that we breathe relief at having matters taken out of our hands.

Such a moment came this morning with the thought—the revolution we are engaged in is a lonely revolution, fought out in our own hearts, a struggle between Nature and Grace. It is the most important work of all in which we are engaged.

If we concentrate our energies primarily on that; then we can trust those impulses of the Holy Spirit and follow them simply, without question. We can trust and believe that all things will work together for good to them that love God, and that he will guide and direct us in our work. We will accomplish just what he wishes us to accomplish and no more, regardless of our striving. Since we have good will, one need no longer worry as though the work depended just on ourselves.

THE CATHOLIC WORKER, DECEMBER 1934

Christ's Lavishness

The usual rather futile comment of the comfortable is—"We know something has to be done—but what can we do about it"—and they are uncomfortable in their comfort and if they are blessed with a conscience, they suffer without knowing what to do about it.

And above all, be generous—and lavish. Christ is lavish with his gift to us—why should we fear to be extravagant in return? Do not say to yourself, "where will it all end, if I start this?"

THE CATHOLIC WORKER, FEBRUARY 1935

Liturgy for Life

Living the liturgical day as much as we are able, beginning with prime, using the missal, ending the day with compline and so going through the liturgical year we find that it is now not us, but Christ in us, who is working to combat injustice and oppression. We are on our way to becoming "other Christs." We cannot build up the idea of the apostolate of the laity without the foundation of the liturgy.

THE CATHOLIC WORKER, JANUARY 1936

Concern for the "Least of These"

All Americans indeed should wake to reality, and in recalling what Thomas Jefferson stood for in the minds of his countrymen, look around them and contemplate the state we are in today. This issue of the paper is carrying stories of conditions throughout the world.

Inasmuch as we do not concern ourselves with such conditions, we are responsible for them. "Inasmuch as ye have done it unto the least of them ye have done it unto me," Christ said.

THE CATHOLIC WORKER, OCTOBER 1936

Even a Torn Sweater Has Some Warmth Left

It does not matter how old the garment is. A torn sweater, worn-out in the sleeves, still has a great deal of warmth in it, and the warmth of gratitude with which it is received should be felt by those kind readers who remember us in this way.

THE CATHOLIC WORKER, OCTOBER 1936

On the Waterfront

As I waited for the traffic light to change on my way to the Seamen's Defense Committee headquarters, I was idly saying my rosary, which was handy in my pocket. The recitation was more or less automatic, when suddenly like a bright light, like a joyful thought, the words Our Father pierced my heart. To all those who were about me, to all the passersby, to the longshoremen idling about the corner, black and white, to the striking seamen I was going to see, I was akin, for we were all children of a common Father, all creatures of One Creator, and Catholic or Protestant, Jew or Christian, Communist or non-Communist, were bound together by this tie. We cannot escape the recognition of the fact that we are all brothers. Whether or not a man believes in Jesus Christ, his Incarnation, his life here with us, his Crucifixion and Resurrection; whether or not a man believes in God, the fact remains that we are all children of one Father.

Meditation on this fact makes hatred and strife between brothers the more to be opposed. The work we must do is strive for peace and concordance rather than hatred and strife.

THE CATHOLIC WORKER, NOVEMBER 1936

We Are Guilty

*E*very morning now about four hundred men come to Mott Street to be fed. The radio is cheerful, the smell of coffee is a good smell, the air of the morning is fresh and not too cold, but my heart bleeds as I pass the lines of men in front of the store which is our headquarters. The place is packed—not another man can get in—so they have to form in line. Always we have hated lines and now our breakfast which we serve, of cottage cheese and rye bread and coffee, has brought about a line. It is an eyesore to the community. This little Italian village which is Mott Street and Hester Street, this little community within the great city has been invaded by the Bowery, by the hosts of unemployed men, by no means derelicts, who are trying to keep body and soul together while they look for work. It is hard to say, matter-of-factly and cheerfully, "Good morning," as we pass on our way to Mass. It was the hardest to say Merry Christmas, or Happy New Year, during the holiday time, to these men with despair and patient misery written on many of their faces.

One felt more like taking their hands and saying, "Forgive us—let us forgive each other! All of us who are more comfortable, who have a place to sleep, three meals a day, work to do—we are responsible for your condition. We are guilty of each other's sins. We must bear each other's burdens. Forgive us and may God forgive us all!"

THE CATHOLIC WORKER, FEBRUARY 1937

Feeding the Forgotten

Every morning still hundreds of men, sometimes two hundred and sometimes as many as five hundred, come to us to be fed. They are the lame, the halt, the blind. Some are the unemployed, and some are the unemployable. From all over, men drift into New York for work or for food and while employment is picking up to some extent (aside from the tens of thousands of WPA workers being fired). New York will always have her street of forgotten men. Too often the attitude is "You can't do anything with them, so why feed them?" Which is an atheist attitude, since we must see Christ in each man who comes to us. Remember Lazarus who sat at the gate, nursing his sores! The modern social worker would wonder why he didn't go to the clinic to get fixed up and rehabilitated, but our Lord only pointed to the moral that the rich man at whose gate he sat did not feed him.

These men are God's creatures and we must

feed them unquestioningly, with warmth and with hospitality. We cut down our paper this month to four pages because we cannot pay the printing bill, but people are more important than papers.

THE CATHOLIC WORKER, AUGUST 1937

Christ the Worker

And everywhere I have been meeting the unemployed—around the steel mills, the employment agencies, the waterfronts, around the "skid rows" and Bowerys of this country, out in the rural districts where the sharecroppers and tenant farmers face lean months of hunger....Because it is a battle, and because you are not weaklings, we fight our own inclinations to feed only bodies to the small extent we can and let this editorial go. But it is a battle to hang on to religion when discouragement sets in. It is a battle to remember that we are made in the image and likeness of God when employers, treating you with less consideration than animals, turn you indifferently away. It is a fierce battle to maintain one's pride and dignity, to remember that we are brothers of Christ, who ennobled our human nature by sharing it.

But that very thought should give courage and should bring hope.

Christ, the Son of Man, lived among us for thirty-three years. For many of those years he lived in obscurity. When he was a baby, his foster father had to flee with him into Egypt. Joseph was a carpenter, a common laborer, and probably had no more savings than the majority of workers. When he tramped the long weary road, in the heat and dust of the deserts, he, too, and Mary and the Child were doubtless hungry. Do any of those hitchhikers, fleeing from the dust bowl in southern California across mountain and desert, remember, as they suffer, the flight into Egypt?...Christ was a worker and in the three years he roamed through Palestine he had no place to lay his head. But he said, "Take no thought for what ye shall eat and where ye shall sleep, or what ye shall put on. Seek ye first the Kingdom of God and his righteousness and all these things shall be added unto you...For your Heavenly Father knoweth that you have need of these things."

THE CATHOLIC WORKER, DECEMBER 1937

Look On the Face of Christ

The long line of men begins every morning at five-thirty. I can hear them coughing and talking under my window as I wake up, and see the reflection of the flames cast on the walls of my room from the fire they build in the gutter to keep warm. Many of the men bring boxes and bits of wood to cast on it, and as the line moves up, the men get a chance to warm themselves. Many of the men have no overcoats or sweaters. It is good to see that fire as I go down to Transfiguration Church to Mass. The flames are brilliant against the dark street and the sky is purple in contrast. There is never so much color during the day....I told him that I believed most certainly that if public relief stopped, there would be bread riots in the streets. But the men see our own poverty. They know we eat the same breakfast they do. So if we had to stop, they would come, that sad morning, and receiving the tragic message, would go their way, dejected, cold and empty of body and soul....But patient, with the unbearably pathetic patience of the poor. There would be sadness in the thought of no more cheerful fires, no more moments of keen appetite and expectancy. For strangely enough, you do sense that the line is cheerful with that perfectly natural cheerfulness of the moment, that comes with the thought of hot coffee. Even the heavy dull rains of November could not kill that small glow of human comfort that they feel at the knowledge that in a short time, as the line moved along, there would be the keen joy of hunger momentarily assuaged and a trembling body warmed.

I do not believe for one minute that we will have to stop our line. How can we lack faith when we can say each morning after Mass, "Look on the face of Thy Christ"—Christ presents in us in his humanity and Divinity at that moment and is present in the least of his children.

THE CATHOLIC WORKER, DECEMBER 1937

Houses of Hospitality

But we must recognize the hard fact, that no matter how good a social order, there will always be the lame, the halt and the blind who must be helped, those poor of Christ, the least of his children, whom he loved, and through whom there is a swift and easy road to find him.

With Houses of Hospitality growing up all over the country, we emphasize again that in spite of the need of centers for indoctrination, meetings and the distribution of literature, the ideal is personal responsibility. When we succeed in persuading our readers to take the homeless into their homes, having a Christ room in the house as Saint Jerome said, then we will be known as Christians because of the way we love one another. We should have hospices in all the poor parishes. We should have coffee lines to take care of the transients; we should have this help given sweetened by mutual forbearance and Christian charity. But we need more Christian homes where the poor are sheltered and cared for....So we do not cease to urge more personal responsibility on the part of those readers who can help in this way. Too often we are afraid of the poor, of the worker. We do not realize that we know him, and Christ through him, in the breaking of bread.

THE CATHOLIC WORKER, FEBRUARY 1938

The Little We Can Do

There is always the complaint—"but we are only feeding them!" from some members of the groups in different parts of the country. It is right never to be satisfied with the little we can do, but we must remember the "little way" of Saint Thérèse—we must remember the importance of giving even a drink of cold water in the name of Christ.

THE CATHOLIC WORKER, MARCH 1938

Active Force of Love

We are afraid of the word love and yet love is stronger than death, stronger than hatred. If we do not emphasize the law of love, we betray our trust, our vocation. We must stand opposed to the use of force.

Saint Paul, burning with zeal, persecuted the church. But he was converted. Again and again in the history of the Church, the conquered overcome the conquerors.

We are not talking of passive resistance. Love and prayer are not passive but a most active glowing force.

And we ask with grief who are they amongst us

who pray with faith and with love, and so power-
fully that they can move the mountains of hatred
that stand in our path. The soul needs exercise as
well as the body and if we do not exercise our soul
in prayer now, we will be puny and ineffectual in
the trials that await us.

THE CATHOLIC WORKER, SEPTEMBER 1938

Hospitality for All

We believe it most necessary to give a sense
of family life to those who come to us. We believe
a sense of security is as necessary as bread or
shelter. We believe that when we undertake the
responsibility of caring for a man who comes to us,
we are accepting it for good. We know that men
cannot be changed in a day or three days, nor in
three months. We are trying "to make men." And
this cannot be done overnight. Some, indeed, are
shiftless and some dishonest; but our aim is to try
to see Christ in these men and to change them by
our love for them; and the more hopeless a case
seems the more we are driven to prayer, which as
it should be....There is so much to do and we
never feel that the work is done right, or that we
give enough to each other's problems....

Living as we do in the midst of thousands,

almost in the streets, I am often reminded of our quest: "I will arise and go about the city: in the streets and broad ways I will seek him whom my soul loveth.

"I sought him and found him *not*....But, when I had a little passed by them, I found him whom my soul loveth: I held him and I will not let him go." We must, all of us, pass by these works of ours, because if we don't find him and hold him, how are we to bring him to the others?

THE CATHOLIC WORKER, SEPTEMBER 1939

Community of Poverty

*O*ur poverty is not a stark and dreary poverty, because we have the security which living together brings. But it is that very living together that is often hard....It is the work of our time which every Catholic must be engaged in as much as he can. There is no one who could not make more sacrifices to feed the poor, to clothe the naked. To follow Christ we have got to aim to be poor as he was....

When the burdens pile high and the weight of all the responsibilities we have undertaken bows us down, when there are never enough beds to go around and never enough food on the table, then it is good to sit out in the cool of the evening with all our neighbors and exchange talk about babies and watch the adventurous life of the street.

The world is bowed down with grief, and in many ways God tries to bring us joy and peace. They may seem at first to be little ways but if our hearts are right they color all our days and dispel the gray of the sadness of the times.

THE CATHOLIC WORKER, SEPTEMBER 1939

Community of Prayer

And now Advent is upon us and we must begin to fast. We read (in a Hearst paper!) picked up from a subway seat, that the Holy Father is beginning a week's vigil for peace, spending the time in prayer and fasting. Rabbis and ministers of New York City, according to the story, are joining with him in prayer. It gives one a sense of great loyalty and devotion to our Holy Father when we hear of his storming Heaven with his supplications. We want to join him, to add our prayers and sacrifices to his. Last Lent our priest in the Precious Blood Church around on Baxter Street was enjoining us all to fast. "Too much eatings, and too much drinkings!" he told us sternly. And too little prayer.

THE CATHOLIC WORKER, DECEMBER 1939

Part Two

THE FORTIES:
THE WAR YEARS

Food for the Soul

This work of ours toward a new heaven and a new earth shows a correlation between the material and the spiritual, and, of course, recognizes the primacy of the spiritual. Food for the body is not enough. There must be food for the soul. Hence the leaders of the work, and as many as we can induce to join us, must go daily to Mass, to receive food for the soul. And as our perceptions are quickened, and as we pray that our faith be increased, we will see Christ in each other, and we will not lose faith in those around us, no matter how stumbling their progress is. It is easier to have faith that God will support each House of Hospitality and Farming Commune and supply our needs in the way of food and money to pay bills than it is to keep a strong, hearty, living faith in each individual around us—to see Christ in him. If we lose faith, if we stop the work of indoctrinating, we are in a way denying Christ again.

We must practice the presence of God. He said that when two or three are gathered together, there he is in the midst of them. He is with us in our kitchens, at our tables, on our bread lines, with our visitors, on our farms. When we pray for our material needs, it brings us close to his humanity. He, too, needed food and shelter. He, too, warmed his hands at a fire and lay down in a boat to sleep.

THE CATHOLIC WORKER, FEBRUARY 1940

Love Not Death

*I*nstead of gearing ourselves in this country for a gigantic production of death-dealing bombers and men trained to kill, we should be producing food, medical supplies, ambulances, doctors and nurses, for the works of mercy, to heal and rebuild a shattered world....We are urging what is a seeming impossibility—a training to the use of non-violent means of opposing injustice, servitude and a deprivation of the means of holding fast to the Faith. It is again the Folly of the Cross. But how else is the Word of God to be kept alive in the world. That Word is Love, and we are bidden to love God and to love one another. It is the whole law, it is all of life. Nothing else matters. Can we do this best in the midst of such horror as has been going on these past months by killing, or by offering our lives for our brothers?

THE CATHOLIC WORKER, JUNE 1940

Agony of the Poor

Our greatest misery is our poverty which gnaws at our vitals, which is an agony to the families in our midst. And the only thing we can do about it is to appeal to you, our readers, begging your help. And how many of our readers are away or who have extra responsibilities in summer! Those of you who read this, those of you who have helped us before, please help us. We are stewards, and we probably manage very badly in trying to take care of all those who come, the desperate, the dispossessed. Like Peter, they say, "To whom else shall we go?" and they are our brothers in Christ. They are more than that, they are Christ appearing to you. So please help us to keep going. Help these suffering members of the sorrowing Body of Christ.

THE CATHOLIC WORKER, JULY-AUGUST 1940

The Weakness of War

The leaders of thought have failed the people because they have lost touch with the common man. They have lived in ivory towers; they have made themselves gross and comfortable. They have sacrificed their integrity for a mess of pottage. They have trusted to mass movements and mass responses and have not appealed to personalist response. They have trusted to words, ideas—they have not gone to the worker as Pope Pius XI appealed; they have not led by example. Or in those cases where they have gone to the workers they have been discouraged at finding the same vices and greed and dishonesty among the poor, and, looking for quick results, have become discouraged and aloof.

And war has come upon the world, and they have turned everywhere to the use of force, compulsion, denying freedom....

If we love our fellows, we have faith in them. But the loss of faith in men is epitomized now by the war spirit throughout the world, the belief that only force can overcome force. That only by war can we retain freedom and escape from the slavery of the totalitarian states. That men are not strong enough spiritually to use good means, so they are compelled to use evil means....

But we cannot lose hope, just as we cannot lose faith in the teaching and examples of Jesus Christ. We know that men are but dust, but we know too that they are little less than the angels. We know them to be capable of high heroism, of sacrifice, of endurance. They respond to this call in wartime. But the call is never made to them to oppose violence with non-resistance, a strengthening of the will, an increase in love and faith.

THE CATHOLIC WORKER, SEPTEMBER 1940

Oppose War

We say, frankly, that we wish indeed the workers would lay down their tools and refuse to make the instruments of death. We wish that they were so convinced of the immorality of modern wars that they would refuse to make the instruments of those wars.

THE CATHOLIC WORKER, APRIL 1941

Manual Labor: Foundation of Work

*W*e should write more about manual labor. It's another one of the foundation stones of the work, of the social edifice we are trying to build. Manual labor, voluntary poverty, works of mercy, these are means of reaching the workers and learning from them, and teaching them. Besides inducing cooperation, besides overcoming barriers and establishing the spirit of brotherhood (besides just getting things done), manual labor enables us to use our body as well as our hands, our minds. Our bodies are made to be used, just as they are made to be respected as temples of the soul. God took on our human flesh and became man. He shared our human nature. He rose from the dead and his disciples saw the wounds in his hands, his feet and his side. They saw his body, that it was indeed a body still. He was not a disembodied spirit. We believe in the resurrection of the body, free from fatigue, from pain and disease and distortion and deformities, a glorified body, a body transfigured by love. All these are reasons for respecting the body, and using it well, not neglecting it by disuse.

THE CATHOLIC WORKER, MAY 1941

Spiritual Work

You say you are not much use as a Catholic Worker, lying there on your bed through the long years. But when it comes to work, physical work is hard, but mental work is harder, and spiritual work is hardest of all. You cannot use your hands to write, nor your eyes to read, but there are all the faculties of the soul you can be using, and as you lie there you can move mountains. You may not see them move it may be a mountain on the other side of the world or in Chile.

THE CATHOLIC WORKER, OCTOBER 1941

"Sentimentality" of Suffering

Another Catholic newspaper says it sympathizes with our sentimentality. This is a charge always leveled against pacifists. We are supposed to be afraid of the suffering, of the hardships of war.

But let those who talk of softness, of sentimentality, come to live with us in cold, unheated houses in the slums. Let them come to live with the criminal, the unbalanced, the drunken, the degraded, the pervert. (It is not decent poor, it is not the decent sinner who was the recipient of

Christ's love.) Let them live with rats, with vermin, bedbugs, roaches, lice (I could describe the several kinds of body lice).

Let their flesh be mortified by cold, by dirt, by vermin; let their eyes be mortified by the sight of bodily excretions, diseased limbs, eyes, noses, mouths.

Let their noses be mortified by the smells of sewage, decay and rotten flesh. Yes, and the smell of the sweat, blood and tears spoken of so blithely by Mr. Churchill, and so widely and bravely quoted by comfortable people.

Let their ears be mortified by harsh and screaming voices, by the constant coming and going of people living herded together with no privacy. (There is no privacy in tenements just as there is none in concentration camps.)

Let their taste be mortified by the constant eating of insufficient food cooked in huge quantities for hundreds of people, the coarser foods, the cheaper foods, so that there will be enough to go around; and the smell of such cooking is often foul.

Then when they have lived with these comrades, with these sights and sounds, let our critics talk of sentimentality.

THE CATHOLIC WORKER, FEBRUARY 1942

Love Is a Breaking of Bread

Remember the story of Christ meeting his disciples at Emmaus? All along the road he had discoursed to them, had expounded the scriptures. And then they went into the inn at Emmaus, and sat down to the table together. And he took bread and blessed it and broke it and handed it to them, and they knew him in the breaking of bread (Luke 24:13–35).

Love is not the starving of whole populations. Love is not the bombardment of open cities. Love is not killing, it is the laying down of one's life for one's friend.

THE CATHOLIC WORKER, FEBRUARY 1942

The Rosary and the Fist

But that fundamental principle of personalism, the liberty of Christ, example rather than coercion, love rather than hate, the folly of the Cross, serving rather than being served, taking the least place, will continue to be stressed in these sheets. From the first issue of *The Catholic Worker* we have opposed the use of force....

If we do not work out our program on these lines we might as well turn to revolution. "In one

hand the rosary, the other—the clenched fist," as
Michael Quill was reported to have said.

THE CATHOLIC WORKER, FEBRUARY 1942

Spiritual Neglect

It is true that much hero worship is
misplaced, exaggerated, even hysterical. But it is
also true that war makes the common soldier
realize the tremendous adventurous capabilities of
man. Farm boys, laborers, the man in the street is
suddenly trained to fly the ocean, to risk his life
daily. What is cheered as remarkable in one in
peace time is expected of the multitude in time of
war. Grueling hours, constant work, in medical
corps, in kitchen police, often heroic sacrifice
(these are times when by compulsion soldiers are
expected in theory to practice the counsels of
poverty, obedience and chastity. If you speak
openly of the tolerated and organized brothels and
saloons situated near the huge camps, you are
traitorous....). And if the physical capabilities of
our citizens is tapped to such a degree, then what
about the spiritual? They have been consistently
neglected, and neglected, too, by our churchmen.

THE CATHOLIC WORKER, APRIL 1942

Draft Resisting

I will not register for conscription, if conscription comes for women, nor will I make a statement to the government on registration day as to my stand, lest this be used as involuntary registration on my part. Instead, I publish my statement here, my declaration of purpose, and if it encourages other women not to register, I shall be glad at such increase in our numbers.

I shall not register because I believe modern war to be murder, incompatible with a religion of love. I shall not register because registration is the first step towards conscription, and I agree with Cardinal Gasparri that the only way to do away with war is to do away with conscription.

But now in these days it would be desirable to go even further, as did Thoreau, to refuse even the taxes which were to be used to pay for the means to kill our fellow man. In many cases, however, it is all but impossible to separate the tax from the cost of the commodity needed to maintain life....Lord God, teach us in this holy season, to seek the wisdom of poverty. Take away from us our hearts of stone and give us hearts of flesh so that we may grow in love for thee and for our fellows. Amen.

THE CATHOLIC WORKER, JANUARY 1943

See Christ Everywhere

A friend sent us a dollar yesterday, and with it the remark: "Enclosed is for bread, but not to make bums out of those who should be earning their own."

I thought of that this morning when I passed a little group of four who always seem to be hanging around the place, out in front, in the coffee room, in the doorways. Always drunk, sometimes prostrate on the sidewalk, sometimes sitting on the curb, they give a picture of despair or hilarity, according to the mood they are in. And, to the minds of many of our friends, they epitomize the six hundred or so who come here to eat every day.

This morning as I came from Mass, I passed the little vegetable woman around the corner, washing her mustard greens in a huge barrel of cold water. Her hands were raw and cold. It was one of those grey mornings, wet and misty, and the pavement was slimy under foot. I commiserated with her over her hands, and she said: "What are you going to do? If you don't work, you don't eat."

When I passed this same little knot of men in front of the house, whom I had passed on the way to church, I told them about the little Italian woman, and they hung their heads sheepishly and

went away. I don't know what can be done—
except to pray. Here are the most humiliated of
men, the most despised, the evidence of their sins
is flagrant and ever present. And as to what
brought them to this pass—war and poverty,
disease and sorrow—who can tell? Why question?
We must see Christ everywhere, even in his most
degraded guise.

We take care of men by the tens of thousands
during the course of the year, and there is no time
to stop and figure who are the worthy or who are
the unworthy. We are, each of us, unprofitable
servants. We are guilty of each other's sins....

The harvest is great and the laborers are few.
However, the Lord told us to pray for laborers, and
he would send them, so there is something we can
do about it.

THE CATHOLIC WORKER, APRIL 1943

Showing Our Love for the God We Cannot See

It certainly is a solution to the world's
problems, this idea of looking around to see what
you can do for those around you, a true expression
of the second commandment, and the only way

we have of showing our love for God whom we have not seen, but our love for those whom we do see. "Love is an exchange of gifts." And "love is the measure by which we shall be judged."

THE CATHOLIC WORKER, DECEMBER 1942

Dying to Self

To some the word mortification is repellent. But it is dying to self in order to live for others. Saint Paul wrote, "always bearing about in our body the mortification of Jesus that the life also of Jesus may be made manifest in our bodies." It is love that gives these desires and love is a glowing, happy thing, a radiant warming fire. We want to strip ourselves to clothe others. We want to fast because of the hunger of others, and if we cannot feed them, we will share their sufferings....

This blindness of love, this folly of love—this seeing Christ in others, everywhere, and not seeing the ugly, the obvious, the dirty, the sinful—this means we do not see the faults of others, only our own. We see only Christ in them. We have eyes only for our beloved, ears for his voice....

THE CATHOLIC WORKER, JUNE 1944

By Little and by Little We Proceed

Love of brother means voluntary poverty, stripping one's self, putting off the old man, denying one's self, etc. It also means non-participation in those comforts and luxuries which have been manufactured by the exploitation of others. While our brothers suffer, we must compassionate them, suffer with them. While our brothers suffer from lack of necessities, we will refuse to enjoy comforts....And we must keep this vision in mind, recognize the truth of it, the necessity for it, even though we do not, cannot, live up to it. Like perfection. We are ordered to be perfect as our heavenly Father is perfect, and we aim at it, in our intention, though in our execution we may fall short of the mark over and over. Saint Paul says, it is by little and by little that we proceed.

THE CATHOLIC WORKER, DECEMBER 1944

Our Responsibility

To feed the hungry, clothe the naked and shelter the harborless without also trying to change the social order so that people can feed, clothe and shelter themselves is just to apply palliatives. It is to show a lack of faith in one's fellows, their responsibilities as children of God, heirs of heaven.

Of course, "the poor we will always have with us." That has been flung in our teeth again and again, usually with the comment, "so why change things which our Lord said would always be?" But surely he did not intend that there would be quite so many of them. We also have to repeat that line now that war is on and there is plentiful occupation....

Yes, the poor have been robbed of the good material things of life, and when they asked for bread, they have been given a stone. They have been robbed of a philosophy of labor. They have been betrayed by their teachers and their political leaders. They have been robbed of their skills and made tenders of the machine. They cannot cook; they have been given the can. They cannot spin or weave or sew—they are urged to go to Klein's and get a dress for four ninety-eight....

The first unit of society is the family. The family should look after its own and, in addition, as the early fathers said, "every home should have a Christ room in it, so that hospitality may be practiced." "The coat that hangs in your closet belongs to the poor." "If your brother is hungry, it is your responsibility."

"When did we see thee hungry, when did we see thee naked?" People either plead ignorance or they say, "It is none of my responsibility." But we are all members one of another, so we are obliged in conscience to help each other.

THE CATHOLIC WORKER, FEBRUARY 1945

Silence and Prayer

Thoughts on holy silence: Saint Gregory kept silence during Lent. Holy Abbot Agatho for three years carried a pebble in his mouth to gain the virtue of silence....

Prayer is what breath is to the body. Prayer is the hand of the body, waits on it, feeds it, washes it, tends it—as the hands do everything, so pray. "If Stephen had not prayed," writes Saint Augustine, "the Church would never have had Saint Paul."

THE CATHOLIC WORKER, MARCH 1945

Rejoice!

The poor know how to rejoice, we are glad to say, just as profoundly as they know how to suffer.

THE CATHOLIC WORKER, SEPTEMBER 1945

Love

The great need of the human heart is for love, and especially do women's lives seem empty if they are deprived of their own to love. Indeed, we know that the first commandment is to love, and we show our love, as Saint Teresa said, for our God by our love for our fellows. And that is why a great emphasis must be placed on the works of mercy....

In these days of sore distress our happiness and our love will be in doing these things, and in doing these things we will find God and find happiness. As Saint Augustine says: "It is with no doubtful knowledge, Lord, but with utter certainty that I love you. You have stricken my heart with your word, and I have loved you. And indeed heaven and earth and all that is in them tell me wherever I look that I should love you. Not the beauty of any bodily thing, nor the order of the seasons; not the brightness of light that rejoices the eye, nor the sweet melodies of all songs, nor the sweet fragrance of flowers and ointment and spices, not manna, nor honey, not the limbs that carnal love embraces. None of these things do I love in loving my God. Yet in a sense I do love light and melody and fragrance and food and embrace when I love God—the light and the voice and the fragrance and the food, and embrace in the soul, when that shines upon my soul which no place can contain, that voice sounds which no tongue can take from me, I breathe that fragrance which no wind scatters.

"I eat the food which is not lessened by eating, and I lie in that embrace which satiety never comes to sunder. That is what I love, when I love my God."

THE CATHOLIC WORKER, NOVEMBER 1945

Room for Christ

It is no use to say that we are born two thousand years too late to give room to Christ. Nor will those who live at the end of the world have been born too late. Christ is always with us, always asking for room in our hearts.

But now it is with the voice of our contemporaries that he speaks, with the eyes of store clerks, factory workers and children that he gazes; with the hands of office workers, slum dwellers and suburban housewives that he gives. It is with the feet of soldiers and tramps that he walks, and with the heart of anyone in need that he longs for shelter. And giving shelter or food to anyone who asks for it, or needs it, is giving it to Christ....

If we hadn't got Christ's own words for it, it would seem raving lunacy to believe that if I offer a bed and food and hospitality for Christmas—or any other time, for that matter—to some man, woman or child.

THE CATHOLIC WORKER, DECEMBER 1945

The Stranger's Room

Some time ago I saw the death notice of a sergeant-pilot who had been killed on active service. After the usual information, a message was added which, I imagine, is likely to be imitated. It said that anyone who had ever known the dead boy would always be sure of a welcome at his parents' home. So, even now that the war is over, the father and mother will go on taking in strangers for the simple reason that they will be reminded of their dead son by the friends he made.

That is rather like the custom that existed among the first generations of Christians, when faith was a bright fire that warmed more than those who kept it burning. In every house then a room was kept ready for any stranger who might ask for shelter; it was even called "the stranger's room": and this not because these people, like the parents of the dead airman, thought they could trace something of someone they loved in the stranger who used it, not because the man or woman to whom they gave shelter reminded them of Christ, but because—plain and simple and stupendous fact—he was Christ.

THE CATHOLIC WORKER, DECEMBER 1945

Atonement

In Christ's human life there were always a few who made up for the neglect of the crowd. The shepherds did it, their hurrying to the crib atoned for the people who would flee from Christ.

The wise men did it; their journey across the world made up for those who refused to stir one hand's breadth from the routine of their lives to go to Christ. Even the gifts that the wise men brought have in themselves an obscure recompense and atonement for what would follow later in this Child's life. For they brought gold, the king's emblem, to make up for the crown of thorns that he would wear; they offered incense, the symbol of praise, to make up for the mockery and the spitting; they gave him myrrh, to heal and soothe, and he was wounded from head to foot and no one bathed his wounds. The women at the foot of the cross did it too, making up for the crowd who stood by and sneered.

We can do it, too, exactly as they did. We are not born too late. We do it by seeing Christ and serving Christ in friends and strangers, in everyone we come in contact with. While almost no one is unable to give some hospitality or help to others, those for whom it is really impossible are not debarred from giving room to Christ, because, to take the simplest of examples, in those they live with or work with is Christ disguised. All our life is bound up with other people; for almost all of us happiness and unhappiness are conditioned by our relationship with other people. What a simplification of life it would be if we forced ourselves to see that everywhere we go is Christ, wearing out socks we have to darn, eating the food we have to cook, laughing with us, silent with us, sleeping with us....

THE CATHOLIC WORKER, DECEMBER 1945

Mercy

We must consider our daily occupation in the light of a work of mercy. We must work together.

THE CATHOLIC WORKER, MAY 1946

Visiting the "Disturbed Ward"

*J*ust as we have to see Christ in his most degraded guise, on the Bowerys and skid rows of the country, so we must see the Blessed Mother everywhere too, I read this once, and it is a terrible thing, a hard thing. How hard it is to see her in inmates of a mental hospital for instance, in the "disturbed ward" which is generally the worst ward, and one least visited....

I remembered our horror as children in reading *Jane Eyre*, of the first wife who was mad and confined in an upper room of the house. Since coming in contact with people who have for the time being lost their minds, I have come to the conclusion that given a large house, it is far better for a family to have that locked room for a loved one where a patient can be cared for at home, than putting them out of sight and out of mind. We do not love enough, that is the trouble....

A chaplain told me that it was no use his going to see patients on such wards. I can only feel that more faith and hope are needed. Where there is life there is hope....There is too little visiting the prisoner, too little visiting the sick in mental hospitals. Generally it is regarded as of no use.

THE CATHOLIC WORKER, JUNE 1946

Love Is the Measure

We confess to being fools and wish that we were more so. In the face of the approaching atom bomb test…in the face of an approaching maritime strike; in the face of bread shortages and housing shortages; in the face of the passing of the draft extension, teen-agers included, we face the situation that there is nothing we can do for people except to love them. If the maritime strike goes on there will be no shipping of food or medicine or clothes to Europe or the Far East, so there is nothing to do again but to love. We continue in our fourteenth year of feeding our brother and clothing him and sheltering him and the more we do it the more we realize that the most important thing is to love. There are several families with us, destitute families, destitute to an unbelievable extent and there, too, is nothing to do but to love. What I mean is that there is no chance of rehabilitation, no chance, so far as we see, of changing them; certainly no chance of adjusting them to this abominable world about them, and who wants them adjusted anyway?

THE CATHOLIC WORKER, JUNE 1946

Love Large

*W*hat we would like to do is change the world—make it a little simpler for people to feed, clothe and shelter themselves as God intended them to do....We repeat, there is nothing that we can do but love, and dear God—please enlarge our hearts to love each other, to love our neighbor, to love our enemy as well as our friend.

THE CATHOLIC WORKER, JUNE 1946

Personal Works of Mercy

*E*very house should have a Christ's room. The coat which hangs in your closet belongs to the poor. If your brother comes to you hungry and you say, Go be thou filled, what kind of hospitality is that? It is no use turning people away to an agency, to the city or the state or the Catholic Charities. It is you yourself who must perform the works of mercy.

THE CATHOLIC WORKER, MAY 1947

Destitution

People say, you can't really realize how terrible this is, this destitution. In a way, yes, you do get used to it. It is terrible to admit it, but you do. The first time I saw a bread line with its homeless ones, footsore, wrapped in rags, my heart turned over within me.

You have wounded my heart, my love. Jesus Christ himself said, "I have no place to lay my head." One of the most pointed stories he told of the poor was that of Lazarus sitting at the door of Dives, waiting for crumbs. We are all Dives in a way.

And what if it is their own fault, these poor? What about the story of the prodigal son? How the Father loved him and welcomed him! We can only show our love for Christ by our love for these his least ones. Our food isn't much. We haven't many clothes to give out. But we can keep trying to show our love.

THE CATHOLIC WORKER, JULY-AUGUST 1947

Letter on Hospices

*U*nless the seed fall into the ground and die, itself remaineth alone. But if it die it bringeth forth much fruit. So I don't expect any success in anything we are trying to do, either in getting out a paper, running houses of hospitality or farming groups, or retreat houses on the land. I expect that everything we do be attended with human conflicts, and the suffering that goes with it, and that this suffering will water the seed to make it grow in the future. I expect that all our natural love for each other which is so warming and so encouraging and so much a reward of this kind of work and living will be killed, put to death painfully by gossip, intrigue, suspicion, distrust, etc., and that this painful dying to self and the longing for the love of others will be rewarded by a tremendous increase of supernatural love amongst us all. I expect the most dangerous of sins cropping up amongst us, whether of sensuality or pride it does not matter, but that the struggle will go on to such an extent that God will not let it hinder the work but that the work will go on, because that work is our suffering and our sanctification....

THE CATHOLIC WORKER, JULY-AUGUST 1947

The Fundamentals

What are we trying to do? We are trying to get to heaven, all of us. We are trying to lead a good life. We are trying to talk about and write about the Sermon on the Mount, the Beatitudes, the social principles of the Church and it is most astounding, the things that happen when you start trying to live this way. To perform the works of mercy becomes a dangerous practice....It is a good thing to live from day to day and from hour to hour....We are convinced that the world can be saved only by a return to these ideas: voluntary poverty, manual labor, works of mercy, hospitality. They are fundamental....

We do not feel that we need permission from the clergy or bishops to start a house to practice the works of mercy. If they do not like it, they can tell us to stop and we will gladly do so. But asking them to approve before any work is done is like asking them to assume a certain amount of responsibility for us.

THE CATHOLIC WORKER, JANUARY 1948

A Time of Waiting

Advent is a time of waiting, of expectation, of silence. Waiting for our Lord to be born. A pregnant woman is so happy, so content. She lives in such a garment of silence, and it is as though she were listening to hear the stir of life within her. One always hears that stirring compared to the rustling of a bird in the hand. But the intentness with which one awaits such stirring is like nothing so much as a blanket of silence.

THE CATHOLIC WORKER, DECEMBER 1948

Be Still

In silence we hear so much that is beautiful. The other day I saw a young mother who said, "The happiest hour of the day is that early morning hour when I lie and listen to the baby practicing sounds and words. She has such a gentle little voice...."

To love with understanding and without understanding. To love blindly, and to folly. To see only what is lovable. To think only on these things. To see the best in everyone around, their virtues rather than their faults. To see Christ in them.

THE CATHOLIC WORKER, DECEMBER 1948

Examination

*H*ere is my examination at the beginning of Advent, at the beginning of a new year. Lack of charity, criticism of superiors, of neighbors, of friends and enemies. Idle talk, impatience, lack of self-control and mortification towards self, and of love towards others. Pride and presumption. (It is good to have visitors—one's faults stand out in the company of others.) Self-will, desire not to be corrected, to have one's own way. The desire in turn to correct others, impatience in thought and speech.

The remedy is recollection and silence. Meanness about giving time to others and wasting it myself. Constant desire for comfort. First impulse is always to make myself comfortable. If cold, to put on warmth; if hot, to become cool; if hungry, to eat; and what one likes—always the first thought is of one's own comfort. It is hard for a woman to be indifferent about little material things. She is a homemaker, a cook; she likes to do material things. So let her do them for others, always. Woman's job is to love. Enlarge thou my heart, Lord, that thou mayest enter in.

THE CATHOLIC WORKER, DECEMBER 1948

Natural Rights

*E*very month I shall have to explain the title to this series. We are not expecting Utopia here on this earth. But God meant things to be much easier than we have made them. A man has a natural right to food, clothing, and shelter. A certain amount of goods is necessary to lead a good life. A family needs work as well as bread. Properly is proper to man. We must keep repeating these things. Eternal life begins now....But it is hard to love, from the human standpoint and from the divine standpoint, in a two-room apartment.

THE CATHOLIC WORKER, JULY-AUGUST 1948

To Die for Love

*L*ove must be tried and tested and proved. It must be tried as though by fire, and fire burns. It is a dreadful thing to fall into the hands of a living God.

In times of catastrophe we are all willing to share. In an earthquake, hurricane, war or plague, people begin to love one another.

THE CATHOLIC WORKER, SEPTEMBER 1948

Harrisburg Story

Someday something will happen, someday there will be the climax, the glory, the fullness of life, release, joy and freedom....

How to draw a picture of the strength of love. It seems at times that we need a blind faith to believe in it at all. There is so much failure all about us. It is so hard to reconcile oneself to such suffering; such long-enduring suffering of body and soul that the only thing one can do is to stand by and save the dying ones who have given up hope of reaching out for beauty, joy, ease and pleasure in this life. For all their reaching, they got little of it. To see these things in the light of faith, God's mercy! God's justice! His devouring love!...

What we do is so little. The stink of the world's injustice and the world's indifference is all around us. The smell of the dead rat, the smell of acrid oil from the engines of the Pennsylvania railroad, the smell of boiled bones from Swift's. The smell of dying human beings.

THE CATHOLIC WORKER, OCTOBER 1948

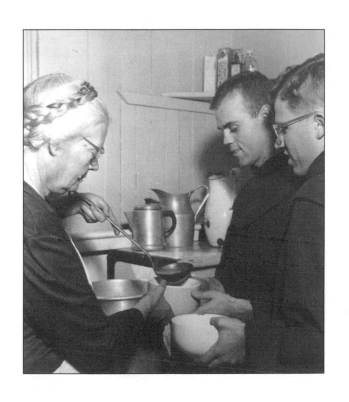

Part Three

THE FIFTIES:
PACIFISM AND THE
ATOMIC BOMB

The Satan Bomb

If we say, any of us, that we do not fear death, which we all must look forward to as a certainty, then we are liars. But it is not death we are supposed to fear, but the judgment, and live accordingly.

THE CATHOLIC WORKER, MARCH 1950

Poverty Incorporated

We must go on with the work. And what is the work but to love God and our neighbor, to show our love for God by our love for our neighbor. When Jesus was asked who was our neighbor he told the story of the good Samaritan. When he pictured the last judgment he listed the corporal works of mercy.

THE CATHOLIC WORKER, MAY 1950

Peace in Community

I do not know how to love God except by loving the poor. I do not know how to serve God except by serving the poor....

Here, within this great city of nine million people, we must, in this neighborhood, on this street, in this parish, regain a sense of community which is the basis for peace in the world.

THE CATHOLIC WORKER, OCTOBER 1950

The Message of Love

One of the saddest and sorriest things about poverty is the envy, hatred, venom and despair suffered by the poor. It is part of their suffering.

THE CATHOLIC WORKER, DECEMBER 1950

Inventory

What a paradox it is, this natural life and this supernatural life. We must give up our lives to gain them, we must die to live, be pruned to bear fruit. We want to be free, and we want to be free of responsibility except for our own. Am I my brother's keeper? Or can I be free when other men are enslaved? We speak in large general terms in our press, but when we talk among ourselves, we talk of our own homes, our own children.

THE CATHOLIC WORKER, JANUARY 1951

Putting on Poverty,
Putting on Christ

We talk about love and we write about love, and love means that we must give and we must suffer. Who is not poor and we are not poor, who does not suffer, and we do not suffer? Love means embracing voluntary poverty too. We have got to begin to be poor. If we try to be poor, we will try to strip ourselves and put on Christ.

THE CATHOLIC WORKER, NOVEMBER 1951

Doing Nothing

It is so hard to sit and do nothing. And yet in many a case that is all one can do. Just listen. And do nothing.

THE CATHOLIC WORKER, JANUARY 1952

Poverty and Precarity

I am convinced that if we had an understanding and a love of poverty we would begin to be as free and joyous as Saint Francis, who had a passion for Lady Poverty and lives on with us in joyous poverty through all the centuries since his death....We must talk about poverty because people lose sight of it, can scarcely believe that it exists.

It is simpler just to be poor. It is simpler to beg. The thing to do is not to hold on to anything....

But the tragedy is that we do, we all do. We hold on to our books, our tools, such as typewriters, our clothes, and instead of rejoicing when they are taken from us, we lament. We protest at people taking time or privacy. We are holding on to these goods. It is a good thing to remember....

Over and over again in the history of the church the saints have emphasized poverty. Every community which has been started has begun in poverty and in incredible hardships by the rank and file priest and brother and monk and nun who gave their youth and energy to good works. And the result has always been that the orders thrived, the foundations grew, property was extended till holdings and buildings were accumulated and although there was still individual poverty, there was corporate wealth. It is hard to keep poor.

THE CATHOLIC WORKER, MAY 1952

Love and Justice

All action springs from love….It is a work of mercy to rebuke the sinner, to comfort the afflicted, to enlighten the ignorant. We must choose what means we can, and they must be pure means….

If we are afraid, we must pray not to be afraid, to be fools for Christ. Love includes justice.

THE CATHOLIC WORKER, JULY-AUGUST 1952

The Long Loneliness

We have all known the long loneliness and we have learned that the only solution is love and that love comes with community.

THE LONG LONELINESS

Poverty Is to Care and Not to Care

Sometimes it takes but one step. We would like to think so. And yet the older I get the more I see that life is made up of many steps, and they are very small affairs, not giant strides. They may loom large in our consciousness, they may look big, but they are but boulders on the way, that we have overcome....

But the daily, hourly, minutely giving up of one's own will and possessions, which means poverty, is a hard, hard thing, and I don't think it ever gets any easier.

You can strip yourself, and you can be stripped, as Koestler wrote in his story of a French concentration camp, but still you are going to reach out like an octopus and seek your own. Your comfort, your ease, your refreshment, and it may mean books and music, the interior senses being gratified, or it may mean food and drink. One giving up is no easier than the other. Cups of coffee, cigarettes, jealousy of time, etc.

These are things we all know about, or should know about. It is a personal affair, such poverty, for the celibate, willing or unwilling....

The only way to live in any security is to live so close to the bottom that when you fall you do not have far to drop, you do not have much to lose....

There have been many sins against the poor which cry out to high heaven for vengeance. The one listed as one of the seven deadly sins is depriving the laborer of his share. There is another one, that is, instilling in him the paltry desires to satisfy that for which he must sell his liberty and his honor. Not that we are not all guilty of concupiscence, but newspapers, radios, television, and battalions of advertising people (woe to that generation) deliberately stimulate his desires, the satisfaction of which mean the degradation of the family.

THE CATHOLIC WORKER, APRIL 1953

Instruments of Salvation

Community is the hardest problem of all. "Sharing" is too often interpreted to mean that what is yours is mine and what is mine is mine....

God has brought us all together to be instruments of each other's salvation and if ever the old man is to be put to death and the New Man, Jesus Christ, put on ("Put ye on therefore the Lord Jesus Christ") it will be done through community. How we should treasure these sufferings, these criticisms, these wounds to vanity and self-esteem! The way we take them is certainly a measure of our pride and selfishness! We can begin to know ourselves, and so to know Thee, O Lord. (That was a prayer of Saint Augustine's.)

THE CATHOLIC WORKER, MAY 1953

Love Is a Warming Fire

This work came about because we started writing of the love man should have for his brother, in order to show his love for God. It's the only way he can know he loves God.

The main thing, of course, is love even to the folly of the Cross.

THE CATHOLIC WORKER, NOVEMBER 1954

Where Are the Poor?

What can we do, what is to be done? First of all, we can admit that our so-called American way of life has meant great inequalities, and that there does indeed exist a great mass of poor and unemployed people who are in need of help in this country as well as abroad. We need to study ways to change the social order, or at least admit to others whose work it is, and who have the time and vocation to do it, that we need a balanced social order, where man will be closer to the land, where there is a possibility of ownership and responsibility, and work for young and old, and that security which ownership in industry would bring. We need to study the idea of credit unions and cooperatives, and small groups to work out the idea of family communities, and village communities, and decentralized living. We need to study as far as we are able, the entire distributist program. But together with this intellectual approach, we need to approach the problem directly, and as Christians....

If we were convinced of the need, if our consciences were aroused, how much could we not do, even those of most modest income, in the way of helping the poor.

THE CATHOLIC WORKER, JANUARY 1955

Prayer and Fasting

We don't realize what great healings of body and soul will follow prayer and fasting, and the almsgiving that goes with fasting.

THE CATHOLIC WORKER, APRIL 1955

The Poor in Prison

Another thing I would like to call attention to is the inhuman crowding. From the outside the Tombs is a great imposing building, but inside we were packed like animals for shipment in cages. We saw these same cages at Delancey Street,

Thirtieth Street and Second Street. We pass by them daily and do not realize that inside are men and women penned, inside there is the weeping and the groaning of despair. What a neglected work of mercy visiting the prisoner.

"When were you in prison, Lord, and we did not visit you?" It is a hard picture Christ presents. He did not forgive this ignorance.

"Inasmuch as you did not visit these prisoners ye did not visit me."

"But they are guilty,
they are the scum of the earth,
they are the refuse, they are the
offscourings. They drink, they take dope,
they are prostitutes. They are vicious
themselves and they make others vicious.
They even sell drugs to little children.
They are where they belong.
Prison is too good for them.
We can't pamper them."

"I have come to call them to repentance.
I have come to be with publicans and sinners.
I have come for the lost sheep. I am more there
with these most miserable ones than with the
judges sitting on the high seats." This is not
sentimentality. This is truth.

Oh yes, one can hear these things very plainly lying in a cell when we were finally permitted to lie down, locked in again in these rows of cages, in a bare stark cell that would outdo the Carmelite in austerity. It was good to kneel there on the floor beside the bed and thank God for the opportunity to be there, to be so stripped of all the earth holds dear to share in some little way the life of prisoners, guilty and innocent, all over the world.

THE CATHOLIC WORKER, JULY-AUGUST 1955

Love Freely Bestowed

God wants man's free service, his freely bestowed love. So we protest and cry out against every infringement of that great gift of God, freedom, our greatest gift, after the gift of life.

That love of brother, that care for his freedom is what causes us to go into such controversial subjects as man and the state, war and peace. The implications of the gospel teaching of the works of mercy lead us into conflict with the powers of this world. Our love of God is a consuming fire. It is a fearful thing to fall into the hands of the living God. It is a living God and a living faith that we are trying to express. We are called to be holy, that is, whole men, in this life of ours. We are trying to follow this call....

We are born alone, we die alone, we must, each one of us, do what we can for God and our brother, not God and country, but God and our Brother, as Christ stated it.

THE CATHOLIC WORKER, NOVEMBER 1955

Work of the Hands

We need to use our hands, to develop skills, to rediscover the sacramentality of things. To whittle, to knit, to crochet, to mold in clay, to weave, to darn or mend also—all of these are the quiet occupations which make for peace.

THE CATHOLIC WORKER, MAY 1956

Goodness Indwelling

There are times in our lives when we feel life flow in our veins, feel ourselves to be alive, we can look into our hearts and find there the Holy Trinity, the indwelling of the Holy Spirit. But we need to be alone, we need to have time, to be at rest, to be rested too....

We need to sleep, we need to rest, we need to lose consciousness, to die in this way, in order to live—and this is on the natural plane. But grace builds on nature, and we must live a good natural life in order to lead the supernatural life to its fullest.

THE CATHOLIC WORKER, JULY-AUGUST 1956

Houses of Hospitality

What does the Catholic Worker mean—what is it?—people often ask. One may answer: voluntary poverty. Another says: an unjudging care for the destitute. Another says: mutual aid; still another: the family. Every House of Hospitality is a family with its faults and virtues, and above all, its love. We can all look at each other and say, "You are bone of my bone and flesh of my flesh," we are all members one of another, since all are members or potential members of the Body of Christ. Even those dread words, pacifism and anarchism, when you get down to it, mean that we try always to love, rather than coerce, "to be what we want the other fellow to be," to be the least, to have no authority over others, to begin with that microcosm man, or rather, with ourselves.

THE CATHOLIC WORKER, NOVEMBER 1957

Remembering the Dead

*D*uring the month of November we are supposed to remember our dead, and sometimes the month is a rainy and dreary one, and it is a sad and mournful duty and brings a pang of the heart, and other times, in the glories of Indian summer, the flowers and golden warmth of the day and the cold crisp nights when walking is good, and sleeping is good, we think not only how good this life is at this dying time of the year, but also how good God is in his promises and reminders of the life to come. We who are oppressed with the certainty of dying are made hopeful by the assurance that "life is changed, not taken away." The trees after their radiant promise of the fall are dead as dead in appearance, and then in the spring, year after year, the tender buds come forth again. We have this promise, repeated over and over again in nature, all the years of our lives, so how can we be sad?

THE CATHOLIC WORKER, NOVEMBER 1957

Loving All

To be a saint is to be a lover, ready to leave all, to give all. Dostoevsky said that love in practice was a harsh and dreadful thing compared to love in dreams, but if "we see only Jesus" in all who come to us; the lame, the halt and the blind, who come to help and to ask for help, then it is easier.

THE CATHOLIC WORKER, APRIL 1958

Heaven Taken by Storm

Already we are receiving letters asking us what the Holy Father means by such a phrase, "even if by force." I find no difficulty in understanding it. Heaven must be taken by violence, and working for a better order here in this world means a terrible struggle. We need all the strength of body and soul and mind too. To live in poverty ourselves, to share the misery, the homelessness, the uncertainty and the precarity of others; to make our protest against the evils of the day, the injustice— to speak out strongly, fearlessly, risking job and home for oneself and for family; enduring the scorn of the world, and often too, of those one loves.

THE CATHOLIC WORKER, NOVEMBER 1958

Lessons of Love

*W*hat very strange encounters come about through the practice of the works of mercy. What strange lessons we learn through this hard way of loving our enemy in the class war which is basic in the world today, very much a part of all the cold war which is going on between the rich and the poor.

THE CATHOLIC WORKER, JANUARY 1959

Retreat

*H*ow far one's vocation will take one is always a mystery, and where one's vocation will take one. But I believe it to be true always that the foundations are always in poverty, manual labor, and in seeming failure. It is the pattern of the Cross, and in the Cross is joy of spirit.

THE CATHOLIC WORKER, AUGUST 1959

Holding Fast

*W*e are all holding fast to this life, no matter how bad it is. It is the only life we know and we keep deluding ourselves that, if we had this or

that, if we had the love we craved, the material
means to develop our talents, we would be happy.

THE CATHOLIC WORKER, NOVEMBER 1959

Building a New Earth

Whether or not men have faith, they cannot
ignore the facts of history, that other men have
lived and died side by side with them in their
desire to educate and do justice as well as show
love for their brothers. The same is true of the
religious minded. They work along spiritual lines,
trying to grow in the spiritual life, deepen their
life of prayer, and too often, the active work of
building a new earth wherein justice dwelleth is
ignored. We are not just souls, we are bodies, and
those poor bodies of desert folk are already
suffering as expellees, refugees, homeless,
transplanted, suffering once again from the
dominating empire-building whites who always
take first place at table, the best of land, and to
whom it has never occurred that they should wash
the feet of their brothers as our Lord showed them
to do.

THE CATHOLIC WORKER, DECEMBER 1959

Part Four

THE SIXTIES:
CIVIL RIGHTS
AND CIVIL
DISOBEDIENCE

Courage and Suffering

*B*efore we reach New Orleans, we stopped at Natchez and before that in Arkansas where we visited Elizabeth Burrow, known to John Cogley, Tom Sullivan and all our Chicago friends in the earliest days of *The Catholic Worker* there. She breaks our hearts with her courage in the face of physical and mental suffering; physical because she has cancer; mental because of the hostility of her people of the South towards the Negro....Visiting Elizabeth, I remembered the words of Thérèse of Lisieux, "Let us suffer if needs be, in bitterness, so long as we suffer." And Elizabeth is "accounted worthy to suffer," as it was said of the apostles in the early days of the Church. Suffering is the strongest of all the spiritual weapons being used in this non-violent revolution going on so slowly in the South.

THE CATHOLIC WORKER, MARCH 1961

Suspect Religion

The motive is love of brother, and we are commanded to love our brothers. If religion has so neglected the needs of the poor and of the great mass of workers and permitted them to live in the most horrible destitution while comforting them with the solace of a promise of a life after death when all tears shall be wiped away, then that religion is suspect. Who would believe such Job's comforters. On the other hand, if those professing religion shared the life of the poor and worked to better their lot and risked their lives as revolutionists do, and trade union organizers have done in the past, then there is a ring of truth about the promises of the glory to come. The cross is followed by the resurrection.

THE CATHOLIC WORKER, SEPTEMBER 1962

True Sharing

Over and over again we are given the chance to re-examine our position—are we ready to relinquish what we have, not just to the poor to share with them what we have but to the poor who rise in revolution to take what they have been deprived of for so long? Are we ready too, to have the drunken poor, the insane poor and what more horrible deprivation than this, to have one's interior senses, the memory, the understanding and the will, impoverished to the extent that one is no longer rational—are we ready to be robbed in this way? Do we really welcome poverty as liberating?

"Let nothing disturb thee, nothing affright thee," Saint Teresa said, "all things are passing, God alone never changes."

Every day we have evidence of his warm loving care for us. Since he has given us his Son—will he not give us also every good thing? All else that we need? We are rich indeed.

THE CATHOLIC WORKER, FEBRUARY 1964

The Mystery of the Poor

On Easter Day, on awakening late after the long midnight services in our parish church, I read over the last chapter of the four gospels and felt that I had received great light and understanding with the reading of them. "They have taken the Lord out of his tomb and we do not know where they have laid him," Mary Magdalene said, and we can say this with her in times of doubt and questioning. How do we know we believe? How do we know we indeed have faith? Because we have seen his hands and his feet in the poor around us. He has shown himself to us in them. We start by loving them for him, and we soon love them for themselves, each one a unique person, most special!...

Most certainly, it is easier to believe now that the sun warms us, and we know that buds will appear on the sycamore trees in the wasteland across from the Catholic Worker office, that life will spring out of the dull clods of that littered park across the way. There are wars and rumors of war, poverty and plague, hunger and pain. Still, the sap is rising, again there is the resurrection of spring, God's continuing promise to us that he is with us always, with his comfort and joy, if we will only ask.

The mystery of the poor is this: That they are Jesus, and what you do for them you do for him. It is the only way we have of knowing and believing in our love. The mystery of poverty is that by sharing in it, making ourselves poor in giving to others, we increase our knowledge of and belief in love.

THE CATHOLIC WORKER, APRIL 1964

Works of Mercy

*T*he works of mercy are works of love. The works of war are works of the devil....

It is voluntary poverty which needs to be preached to the comfortable congregations, so that a man will not be afraid of losing his job if he speaks out on these issues. So that pastors or congregations will not be afraid of losing the support of rich benefactors. A readiness for poverty, a disposition to accept it, is enough to begin with. We will always get what we need. "Take no thought for what you shall eat or drink—the Lord knows you have need of these things."

THE CATHOLIC WORKER, JULY-AUGUST 1964

Joy in Work

*I*t is a joyful experience, to serve the poor, and to be poor ourselves. As our family sits down at the second floor of Saint Joseph's House here on Chrystie Street, folding, labeling and mailing the paper, or as they scrape vegetables on the first floor for our evening meal, each is giving something, sharing with his fellows, no matter how humble his gift. There is therapy in work, and joy in sharing, a sense of belonging for those who are the outcasts of our society.

THE CATHOLIC WORKER, OCTOBER 1964

Who Knows?

Death is always taking us by surprise.

THE CATHOLIC WORKER, NOVEMBER 1964

Prosperity for Some

To go back to the subject of cold. There is an Arab saying "Fire is twice bread." Certainly it is a hard and miserable thing to be cold. It is hard to work. It is hard to keep clean. It is hard to forget the body, this cumbrous instrument of the mind and soul. When the senses are all at peace, satisfied and content, the exercises of the mind and soul seem to be going smoothly. I have thought a good deal along these lines in connection with poverty and destitution and the attitudes of those who suffer these affronts in a prosperous land. I have thought of them when people talk of the demands of labor for higher wages and shorter hours. There have been occasional critical comments about the Catholic

Worker—why do we emphasize these material things? Why are we frozen in these attitudes, these positions about poverty and the social order? It is because we must be like the importunate widow before the unjust judge, like the man who came to borrow some loaves to feed his hungry family and knocked at the door of his friend until he got what he wanted from him.

We emphasize the material because we are working to make that kind of a society in which it is easier for men to be good. And while the triple revolution of automation, civil rights and peace-making is going on, we have to rack our brains, use our imagination, seize upon every opportunity, every encounter, to enlighten our own minds as well as those of others, to inflame our own hearts as well as those of others, that we may all be working for the common good, and towards that Eternal Good for which all hearts long.

THE CATHOLIC WORKER, JANUARY 1965

Holier Than Thou

Of course we consider enlightening the ignorant and counseling the doubtful works of mercy, as indeed they are. As for "rebuking the sinner" we are told not to judge, by our dear Lord, and we are only too conscious of our own all too imperfect state. However, our positions seem to imply a judgment, a condemnation, and we get the "holier than thou" accusation often enough.

THE CATHOLIC WORKER, DECEMBER 1965

Discipline

It is true that we must take ourselves as we are, and recognize that with our education, our families, our backgrounds, it is impossible for us to know what destitution really is. But by attempting self-discipline, reducing our wants, curbing our constant self-indulgence, learning what it means to work by the sweat of our brow, and by enduring the contempt and insult only too often met with, we are learning a kind of poverty.

When we do not recognize the importance ourselves as sons of God, when we do not in faith esteem ourselves and recognize the importance of our work, no matter how small it may seem, we are likely to be crushed by the criticism of others and take refuge in the do-nothing attitude. I once heard a psychiatrist say, man craves recognition more than food or sex and that when he does not get it he feels poor indeed. This is a real poverty to be endured. But it is good to be considered a

fool for Christ, as Saint Paul said, remembering
always the folly of the Cross.

THE CATHOLIC WORKER, JUNE 1966

Simplification

I think most of us wish to be poor, to
simplify our lives, to throw out the trash and make
more room for the good—to put off the old man
and put on the new—to be new creatures, as Saint
Paul said.

THE CATHOLIC WORKER, MARCH-APRIL 1967

Meaningful Work for
the Common Good

In speaking on the works of mercy as direct
action, I have often quoted Father Jimmy
Tompkins, who said that all work should be
considered in the light of the Lord's command to
practice the works of mercy, as expressed in the
twenty-fifth chapter of Saint Matthew. Engineers,
homebuilders, agronomists, chemists, oceanogra-
phers—all have to do with feeding the hungry,
sheltering the homeless, in a long-range plan

which involves the community, the municipality, the state and the nation. It is the individuals who think in terms of pilot projects, and who voice the overall problem of man's need to find meaningful work, creative work for the common good.

THE CATHOLIC WORKER, MARCH-APRIL 1967

Agony Always

One of the early Fathers of the Church once wrote that if we could stand on a mountain top and see all the misery and tragedy of the world, we could not survive the horror of it. Now we have television and can indeed see what is happening, can witness the murder of Lee Harvey Oswald, the torture of prisoners in Vietnam, the death of our own soldiers—horror upon horror, until the mind and soul are blunted, sated with blood, blood which cries out to heaven....

Juliana of Norwich said, and it is for our comfort, "the worst has already happened and been remedied." The worst being the Fall, and the remedy is still with us, "the same yesterday and today and forever." Even today, there are samplings of heaven, in love expressed, in peace maintained.

THE CATHOLIC WORKER, SEPTEMBER 1967

Ignorance No Excuse

Father Paul Hanley Furfey once said to us in a conference that it is obvious from the twenty-fifth chapter of Saint Matthew that God does not forgive ignorance. "When did we see you naked and not cover you, a stranger and never made you welcome? And the Lord will answer, 'I tell you solemnly, insofar as you neglected to do this to one of the least of these, you neglected to do it to me.'"

THE CATHOLIC WORKER, SEPTEMBER 1967

Prodigals

God is on the side even of the unworthy poor, as we know from the story Jesus told of his father and the prodigal son. Charles Peggy, in *God Speaks*, has explained it perfectly. Readers may object that the prodigal son returned penitent to his father's house. But who knows, he might have gone out and squandered money on the next Saturday night, he might have refused to help with the farm work, and asked to be sent to finish his education instead, thereby further incurring his brother's righteous wrath, and the war between the worker and the intellectual, or the conservative and the radical, would be on. Jesus has another answer to that one: to forgive one's brother seventy times seven. There are always answers, although they are not always calculated to soothe.

THE CATHOLIC WORKER, FEBRUARY 1968

Fear in Our Time

It seems to me that we must begin to equal a little bit the courage of the Communists. One of the ways my Communist friends taunt me is by saying, in effect, "People who are religious believe in everlasting life, and yet look how cowardly they are. And we who believe only in this life, see how hard we work and how much we sacrifice. We are not trying to enjoy all this and heaven too. We are willing to give up our life in order to save it."

There is really no answer to this kind of taunt. When I was in Cuba in September 1962, I witnessed what a Franciscan priest, Herve Chaigne, has called an "exemplary" revolution. I felt that it was an example to us in zeal, in idealism and in self-sacrifice and that unless we began to approach in our profession of Christianity some of this zeal of the Communists, we weren't going to get anywhere. But we have to go ahead and think in terms of a third way, not just those two alternatives, capitalism or communism, or my country or the fellowship of all men. We have to begin to see what Christianity really is, that "our God is a living fire; though he slay me yet will I trust him." We have to think in terms of the Beatitudes and the Sermon on the Mount and have this readiness to suffer. "We have not yet resisted unto blood." We have not yet loved our neighbor with the kind of love that is a precept to the extent of laying down our life for him. And our life very often means our money, money that we have sweated for; it means our bread, our daily living, our rent, our clothes. We haven't shown ourselves ready to lay down our life. This is a new precept, it is a new way, it is the new man we are supposed to become. I always comfort myself by saying that Christianity is only two days old (a thousand years are as one day in the sight of God) and so it is only a couple of days that are past and now it is about time we began to take these things literally, to begin tomorrow morning and say, "now I have begun."

THE CATHOLIC WORKER, APRIL 1968

Part Five

THE SEVENTIES:
THE PILGRIMAGE
CONTINUED

Non-Violence at Home

The noon guests are now back to bean soup, pea soup, rice soup and lentil soup and so on....There are two hundred for lunch and perhaps a hundred for supper. Or it might be only fifty. Sometimes it sounds like a multitude because the night crowd are the immediate members of the family and the immediate neighbors round about us who feel at liberty to fight and argue as families will. Nobody gets hurt but there is a good opportunity to practice non-violence. The worst enemies are those of our own household, our Lord once said.

THE CATHOLIC WORKER, JANUARY 1970

Homecoming

I was in Perkinsville to wait with the rest of the family for the return of Eric [Dorothy's grandson] from Vietnam. Two Christmases he had been drafted and was due to report January 2. He was a few months out of high school and his friends had been drafted and some were already in service. He did not grow up in a pacifist atmosphere....And so he went. And now he was coming home. He had written that he was due on

December 19 or 20, and we kept listening for the phone.

One of his friends who had served in Vietnam came in that afternoon looking for Eric, and he spoke of the Vietcong burying thousands alive in Hue. "I know," he said, "I saw those corpses." He spoke defensively as though I, as a pacifist, was on the side of the Vietcong. It is hard to talk to each other, the words of Christianity mean so little, "All men are brothers, God wills that all men be saved. Love your enemy. Deliver me from the fear of my enemies" so that I can be close enough to them to know and love them.

THE CATHOLIC WORKER, JANUARY 1979

On Work and Death

I am reminded of Father Hugo when I write these last words about death because he used to end his delightful, stimulating and provocative retreats with a little dissertation about death. "When your friend comes to you to tempt you to waste your time—'come and let us drink at the neighboring tavern,' tell him, 'Go away, I am dead and my life is hid with Christ in God'" (famous words of Saint Paul).

As he preached his retreats it was often with

enjoyment and humor, but with a deep sense, you felt, of the strong conflict in which we were engaged in our attempts to live a spiritual life. All that we did, work or play, eating or drinking, should be done in the name of the Lord Jesus. Work was co-creative, expiatory, redemptive, and certainly a sharing in the suffering of the world.

THE CATHOLIC WORKER, JANUARY 1970

Always Rebuilding

In war-torn countries rebuilding goes on continually: bridges, homes, schools, churches, destroyed and rebuilt even while shelters are begin also constructed beneath the ground in such long-continuing struggles as that in Vietnam. To let men go hungry and naked and homeless just because of the vastness of the tragedy around us is madness indeed. I am constantly being reminded of the need to keep up our courage and our work, not to give way to useless lethargy.

THE CATHOLIC WORKER, MARCH-APRIL 1970

War of Bitterness, Despair

The work is not without danger—this adventure of ours. We live on a warfront—class war, race war. Mental cases abound, drugged youth haunt our streets and doorsteps. We are, here at First Street, a school of non-violence. Not a week passes when there have not been knives drawn, a fist up-raised, the naked face of hate shown and the silence of bitterness and despair shattered by the crash of breaking crockery or glass, a chair overthrown. But there are other days when suddenly there is laughter, scraps of conversation among the men, and one feels men have been wooed out of their misery for a moment by a sense of comradeship between the young people serving and those served.

THE CATHOLIC WORKER, MARCH-APRIL 1971

Pride in Sacrifice

We run the risk of thinking we're God's gift to humanity, those of us who struggle in our soup kitchens and hospitality houses to be loyal to Him.

SPEECH, SAINT JOSEPH'S HOUSE, 1971 (FROM *DOROTHY DAY: A RADICAL DEVOTION* BY ROBERT COLES)

Attica

I am afraid of what is before us, because
what we sow we will reap. It is an exercise in
courage to write these words, to speak in this way
when it is revolting to consider how much we
profess and how little we perform. God help us.

THE CATHOLIC WORKER, SEPTEMBER 1971

Respect for All

To serve others, to give what we have is not
enough unless we always show the utmost respect
for each other and all we meet.

THE CATHOLIC WORKER, OCTOBER-NOVEMBER 1971

Voluntary Poverty

*S*aint Augustine has some good advice about
voluntary poverty...."Find out how much God has
given you, and from it take what you need; the
remainder which you do not require is needed by
others. The superfluities of the rich are the
necessities of the poor. Those who retain what is
superfluous possess the goods of others."

THE CATHOLIC WORKER, OCTOBER-NOVEMBER 1971

Subtle Forms of Violence

Everywhere there are discussions of non-violence and there is no end to the examination of conscience necessary. Are we violent in our judgement of others? Do we forgive seventy times seven? Do we forgive the jailor, the man who is afraid and uses violence instinctively? Do we forgive the rich, the exploiter? The self-righteous?

THE CATHOLIC WORKER, FEBRUARY 1972

Jail As Protest

We have to accept with humility the fact that we cannot share the destitution of those around us, and that our protests are incomplete. Perhaps the most complete protest is to be in jail, to accept jail, never to give bail or defend ourselves.

THE CATHOLIC WORKER, MAY 1972

Solace From Psalms and Eucharist

It is then that I turn most truly for solace, for strength to endure, to the psalms. I may read them without understanding, and mechanically at first, but I do believe they are the Word, and that Scripture on the one hand and the Eucharist, the Word made Flesh, on the other have in them that strength which no power on earth can withstand.

THE CATHOLIC WORKER, JUNE 1972

Where Justice Dwells

Bread lines are not enough, hospices are not enough. I know we will always have men on the road. But we need communities of work, land for the landless, true farming communes, cooperatives and credit unions. There is much that is wild, prophetic and holy about our work—it is that which attracts the young who come to help us. But the heart hungers for that new social order wherein justice dwelleth.

THE CATHOLIC WORKER, JANUARY 1972

Things Unsaid

"Least said, soonest mended," my mother used to say. We all talk too much and do too little. God help us!

THE CATHOLIC WORKER, JUNE 1973

Pray About Everything

*Y*es, reading is prayer—it is searching for light on the terrible problems of the day, at home and abroad, personal problems and national problems, that bring us suffering of soul and mind and body....There is nothing too small to pray about.

THE CATHOLIC WORKER, JULY-AUGUST 1973

Holding the Father's Hand

*I*t is hard to explain the fact that there is joy in truly religious ceremonies for our departed ones. One has to experience it to know it. They have run their course, they have lived fully, they have encountered and passed through death, that universal experience, that penalty for the Fall, which Christ himself first paid for us all. It indeed can become an occasion of joy, even in anticipation, holding as we can do to our Father's hand.

THE CATHOLIC WORKER, OCTOBER-NOVEMBER 1973

Love Without Asking

Love is an exchange of gifts Saint Ignatius said—maybe he was writing an appeal when he said it. So it is with love I thank you for all your help over years. (You pay God a compliment, Saint Teresa of Ávila says, by asking great things of him.) And God is good. Even without our asking.

THE CATHOLIC WORKER, OCTOBER-NOVEMBER 1973

Religious Principles

We are told by Jesus Christ to practice the works of mercy, not the works of war. And we do not see why it is necessary to ask the government for permission to practice the works of mercy which are the opposite of the works of war. To ask that permission to obey Christ by applying for an exemption [from income tax], a costly and lengthy process, is against our religious principles. It is an interference of the state which we must call attention to again and again.

THE CATHOLIC WORKER, FEBRUARY 1974

Seeing Christ in All

*B*ecause I have been behind bars in police
stations, houses of detention, jails and prison
farms, whatsoever they are called, eleven times,
and have refused to pay federal income taxes and
have never voted, they accept me as an anarchist.
And I, in turn, can see Christ in them even
though they deny Him, because they are giving
themselves to working for a better social order for
the wretched of the earth....God wills that all
men be saved. A hard saying for us to take and
believe and hold to our heart to ease its bitterness.

THE CATHOLIC WORKER, MAY 1974

Reciprocity

*T*he Quakers have a saying, "There is that
which is of God in everyman." In other words,
seeing Christ in each other, as he told us to do.
"Whatever you did for one of my least brethren,
you have done for me." We so often apply these
words to the works of mercy—feeding, clothing
and sheltering others—but those in trouble who
come to the Catholic Worker do the same for us
and each other. The "little" saints like Hans who
taught everyone to bake bread, and Mike who was

so knowledgeable about furnaces and water heaters, and Tom Likely who set tables, cut bread, mixed powdered milk, kept kettles hot, served up teach and coffee to the disconsolate.

THE CATHOLIC WORKER, JUNE 1974

Letting Go

*B*uddhists teach that a man's life is divided into three parts: the first part for education and growing up; the second for continued learning, of course, through marriage and raising a family, involvement with the life of the senses, the mind and spirit; and the third period, the time of withdrawal from responsibility, letting go of the things of life, letting God take over. This is a fragmentary view of the profound teaching of the East. The old saying that man works from sun to sun, but woman's work is never done is a very true one. Saint Teresa wrote of the three interior senses, the memory, the understanding and the will, so even if one withdraws, as I am trying to do from active work, these senses remain active....

THE CATHOLIC WORKER, MARCH-APRIL 1975

A Life Built Around the Works of Mercy

The work Bill Gauchat [follower of Peter Maurin, co-founder of the Catholic Worker] the work of his wife and children, now many of them married and with children of their own, still goes on. He has fed the hungry, clothed the naked. They continue feeding the hungry, clothing the naked, caring for the most helpless. In fact they performed all the works of mercy in one way or another. Their work is a miracle in our day. The Church always includes the spiritual works of mercy as well as the corporal, and when I think of them, I think of the summer schools Bill used to hold on that small farm, during Peter's lifetime, when an altar for Mass was set up in a field, and classes were held, and conferences and discussions went on. This was indeed "enlightening the ignorant, counseling the doubtful, comforting the afflicted," holding up achievable goals which all of us could work for.

THE CATHOLIC WORKER, MAY 1975

Reading vs. Doing

How delightful to read about the spiritual life and how hard to live it.

THE CATHOLIC WORKER, SEPTEMBER 1975

Martyr Complexes

Sometimes life is so hard, we foolishly look upon ourselves as martyrs, because it is almost as though we were literally sharing in the sufferings of those we serve.

THE CATHOLIC WORKER, MAY 1976

Focus

Gregory the Great, who lived around the fifth or sixth century, wisely said that if we pour ourselves too fervently in Church or state affairs, or let ourselves be too upset, we are weakening, or even nullifying, our most potent weapons—the weapons of the spirit.

THE CATHOLIC WORKER, JUNE 1976

Poor in One Way or the Other

We are all poor in one way or another, in soul, mind and body, in exterior or interior goals.

THE CATHOLIC WORKER, OCTOBER-NOVEMBER 1977

The Final Word Is Love

We cannot love God unless we love each other, and to love we must know each other. We know him in the breaking of bread, and we are not alone any more. Heaven is a banquet and life is a banquet, too, even with a crust, where there is companionship.

We have all known the long loneliness and we have learned that the only solution is love and that love comes with community.

THE CATHOLIC WORKER, MAY 1980

Prayer for the Canonization of Servant of God: Dorothy Day

Merciful God, you called your servant Dorothy Day to show us the face of Jesus in the poor and forsaken. By constant practice of the works of mercy, she embraced poverty and witnessed steadfastly to justice and peace. Count her among your saints and lead us all to become friends of the poor ones of the earth, and to recognize you in them. We ask this through your Son, Jesus Christ, bringer of Good News to the poor. Amen.

$\mathscr{B}$IBLIOGRAPHY

Books by Dorothy Day

From Union Square to Rome. New York: Arno Press, 1978, 1938.
House of Hospitality. New York: Sheed & Ward, 1939.
Loaves and Fishes. San Francisco: Harper & Row, 1983, 1963.
The Eleventh Virgin. New York: Albert & Charles Boni, 1924.
The Long Loneliness: The Autobiography of Dorothy Day. San Francisco: Harper & Row, 1981, 1952.
On Pilgrimage. New York: Catholic Worker Books, 1948.
On Pilgrimage: The Sixties. New York: Curtis Books, 1972.
Thérèse. Springfield, Ill.: Templegate, 1979.

Biographies of Dorothy Day

Coles, Robert. *Dorothy Day: A Radical Devotion*. Reading, Mass.: Addison–Wesley, 1987.

Egan, Eileen. *Dorothy Day and the Permanent Revolution*. Erie, Penn.: Benet Press, 1983.

Forest, Jim. *Love Is the Measure: A Biography of Dorothy Day*. New York: Paulist Press, 1986.

Miller, William D. *Dorothy Day: A Biography*. San Francisco: Harper & Row, 1982.

Miller, William D. *A Harsh and Dreadful Love: Dorothy Day and the Catholic Worker Movement*. New York: Liveright, 1973.

O'Grady, Jim. *Dorothy Day: With Love for the Poor*. Staten Island, N.Y.: Ward Hill Press, 1993.

Roberts, Nancy. *Dorothy Day and the Catholic Worker*. Albany: State University of New York Press, 1984.

ABOUT THE AUTHOR

Phyllis Zagano is author of numerous books and articles, including *On Prayer: A Letter for My Godchild* (Liguori Publications, 2001), *Holy Saturday: An Argument for the Restoration of the Female Diaconate in the Catholic Church* (Crossroad, 2000), *Twentieth-Century Apostles: Contemporary Spirituality in Action* (Liturgical Press, 1999).